The History of the Western Movie

The History of the Western Movie

Jem Duducu

WHITE OWL
AN IMPRINT OF PEN & SWORD BOOKS LTD.
YORKSHIRE - PHILADELPHIA

First published in Great Britain in 2025 by
White Owl
An imprint of Pen & Sword Books Limited
Yorkshire – Philadelphia

Copyright © Jem Duducu 2025

ISBN 978 1 03611 591 3

The right of Jem Duducu to be identified as Author of this Work has been asserted by her in accordance with the Copyright, Designs and Patents Act 1988.

A CIP catalogue record for this book is available from the British Library.

All rights reserved. No part of this book may be reproduced, transmitted, downloaded, decompiled or reverse engineered in any form or by any means, electronic or mechanical including photocopying, recording or by any information storage and retrieval system, without permission from the Publisher in writing. NO AI TRAINING: Without in any way limiting the Author's and Publisher's exclusive rights under copyright, any use of this publication to 'train' generative artificial intelligence (AI) technologies to generate text is expressly prohibited. The Author and Publisher reserve all rights to license uses of this work for generative AI training and development of machine learning language models.

Typeset by Mac Style
Printed in the UK by CPI Group (UK) Ltd, Croydon, CR0 4YY.

The Publisher's authorised representative in the EU for product safety is Authorised Rep Compliance Ltd., Ground Floor, 71 Lower Baggot Street, Dublin D02 P593, Ireland.
www.arccompliance.com

For a complete list of Pen & Sword titles please contact

PEN & SWORD BOOKS LIMITED
47 Church Street, Barnsley, South Yorkshire, S70 2AS, England
E-mail: enquiries@pen-and-sword.co.uk
Website: www.pen-and-sword.co.uk
or
PEN AND SWORD BOOKS
1950 Lawrence Road, Havertown, PA 19083, USA
E-mail: uspen-and-sword@casematepublishers.com
Website: www.penandswordbooks.com

*Dedicated to Patricia and Sandy,
the toughest cowgirls this side of the Pecos.*

Contents

Introduction — ix

Chapter 1   In the Beginning — 1

Chapter 2   The Distant Sound of Gunfire — 19

Chapter 3   Filmed in Technicolor — 47

Chapter 4   Code Red — 79

Chapter 5   Oscar Bait — 107

Chapter 6   Post Modernism in the 1800s — 129

Chapter 7   The Big Country on the Small Screen — 149

Chapter 8   A New Century, a New Take — 169

Conclusion — 186

Introduction

In Japan the most popular era of history portrayed in its media is that of the samurai. Admittedly, this covers a vast period of around 850 years, but the interest in and the mythologising of these warriors never goes out of fashion. In Europe, the same can be said of "knights in shining armour", an era that has been a thing of the past for 500 years. America is a country late to the game of nation building, only officially recognised as an independent sovereign state in the Treaty of Paris of 1783, which ended the War of Independence against the British. America has no samurai and no knights, but every country needs its myths and America created theirs with the Western.

Like the samurai and the knights, it all started with the printed word, but because the Western came much later the tone was very different. The Book of Five Rings is an almost philosophical tract written in the 17th century by arguably the greatest samurai swordsman of all time, Miyamoto Musashi. The purpose of the work is to educate so that young samurai could learn from the master. Le Morte d'Arthur by Sir Thomas Mallory is a 15th century retelling of the legend of King Arthur. It purports to be history, but like the Five Rings, it is also designed to explain the tenets of chivalry so that young knights could learn a code of conduct. Le Morte d'Arthur is designed to be a little more entertaining than The Book of Five Rings, but the only people able to read in the 1400s were the aristocracy and clergymen.

But then we come to the second half of the 19th century in America and the "dime novel" (Britain had its own equivalent with the "penny dreadful"). These were mass-produced, cheaply printed books full of lurid details and daring do. They are as fictionalised as Le Morte d'Arthur, but they weren't aimed at aristocrats who were learning a martial code, they were for factory workers, housewives and schoolboys who wanted a bit of frontier glamour in their lives. Writers physically followed the big names of the day. Rumours became history, exaggeration became fact, and tall stories became even bigger. This was not high art or philosophy, it was mass entertainment. But crucially, unlike the samurai or the knights, the American protagonists knew they were being written about and could control the narrative. There was mass market interest in these stories, a phenomenon only just emerging. This was not an iterative change, but a complete game changer.

To continue the comparison, the samurai were almost totally unknown in the West until the 19th century. Knights were not known in Japan until the 20th century. But as soon as the Wild West was created it was marketed globally. In 1883, Bill Cody created Buffalo Bill's Wild West Show. It may have started in Nebraska, but by 1906, it had toured Europe eight times. Queen Victoria saw it, Kaiser Wilhelm II saw it, and the citizens of Europe flooded to it in their tens of thousands. Creators of books, shows, songs and plays were cashing in, so it was only a matter of time before the western frontier would make the leap into that exciting new medium, moving pictures.

By the early years of the 20th century, cinema had been around for a few decades, but the films were mainly novelty footage lasting mere minutes. For more time, energy and, more importantly, money to be spent on these endeavours filmmakers needed to pick a topic that they knew people would pay to see. The stories from the Wild West had proved so popular in other media it was an obvious place to start. These films became known as Westerns, and they are such an intrinsic part of the DNA of Hollywood that if they had never existed the story of the motion picture industry would have been completely different. But because they were there at the beginning, they have remained in the conversation ever since. As Hollywood evolved, so did the Western; when new pressures came to bear on society, these were reflected in the telling of new Westerns. Perhaps surprisingly, the story of the Western is the story of Hollywood more than it is the story of the 19th century.

Chapter 1

In the Beginning

So, what exactly is a Western, a cowboy film, a horse puncher? All are early terms used to describe these movies, but the term Western was first used in a July 1912 magazine article in *Motion Picture World* which referenced films that portray a very specific time and place in western America. The idea of herding cattle on horseback did not originate in America. It was first recorded in Islamic Spain in the Middle Ages, but it's difficult to imagine a Muslim cowboy riding around in the 1300s, stopping periodically to get down from his horse to pray towards Mecca. Where's the hat? The gun? Where's the Americanness of it all?

In film studies, a "Western" is described as a genre, a class of artistic endeavour having a particular form or content. The interesting thing about this genre is that it can encompass action adventures, thrillers, musicals, political allegories, historical epics, horror, comedies and even war films. The genre is very flexible, but the exact definitions get very murky, very quickly. Native American culture was hot in the 1990s, and in 1995 Disney released its animated classic *Pocahontas*, a project that had been started years earlier. That it is animated and has songs are warning signs that the movie will be light on history, but Pocahontas (voiced by First Nation woman Irene Bedard) and John Smith (voiced by the American-but-grew-up-in-Australia, Mel Gibson) were both real, and theirs was a real story which Disney decided to largely ignore.

Pocahontas has white settlers, Native Americans and some action adventure - so is it a Western? Interestingly, nobody considers it to be one, despite the fact that it has many of the usual trappings (although admittedly, there are very few animated Westerns). The problem isn't the music (*Paint Your Wagon*, *Oklahoma!* and *Calamity Jane* will be

2 The History of the Western Movie

discussed later). The film emphasises the idea that Native Americans are as one with nature, the idea personified by the beautifully animated and Oscar winning song "Colors of the Wind". Pocahontas was the daughter of the chief of the Powhatan tribe, and she became, in essence, an ambassador to the English colonial settlement of Jamestown. It was here that she met the English explorer John Smith (forgettable name but interesting guy). So far, so good with the film. But that's it for the history. The two most egregious issues are that we don't see her going to England (where she died and is buried), and at the end of the film, the settlers leave America! That is quite the piece of revisionist history. Another problem is it's set in the early 1600s, so apart from its location in America, in every other way it doesn't really fit the genre's definition.

Killers of the Flower Moon came out in 2023. It's the true story of how, at the start of the 20th century, the Osage people discovered oil on their reservation. In 1921, the federal government passed a law requiring First Nation people to prove "competency" with money. By the early 1920s, the Osage people were the wealthiest in the world per head of population, and white men descended on them like a pack of hungry wolves. In the film, the native language is spoken and native traditions are depicted; there's violence and crime, with a real frontier feel to the locations and amazing performances from Leonardo DiCaprio, Robert De Niro and Lily Gladstone. But nobody called it a Western, even though it fits virtually all the categories of the genre.

The same can be said for Michael Mann's 1992 *Last of the Mohicans* (the ninth film version of this book), where the English are definitely the bad guys (no rehabilitation for them, they are still the perennial villains), with Hawkeye, played by Daniel Day-Lewis, and his Mohawk allies the only voice of reason in a world gone mad. While Wes Studi as Magua (a Native American) is the final bad guy to beat, his motives have been well fleshed out. However, this is one of the rare films set during the Seven Years' War in the mid-1700s (known as the French and Indian War in America). More action, more natives, lots of shooting - but this is the era of colonial America, and it just doesn't feel like "red coats" should be in a Western.

Some Westerns take place during the US Civil War, which is accurate, but a film solely about that conflict would come under the heading of "war film". For example, nobody thinks *Gone with the Wind* is a Western. The geography is all over the place because in the early 1800s the "frontier" of the United States of America was the western border of Illinois, now in the middle of the country. The same can be said of St Louis, then a frontier town, but today nobody would describe St Louis as being in the west of America. So, on the one hand almost everyone knows what a Western is, but on the other, there are no hard and fast rules. To paraphrase United States Supreme Court Justice Potter Stewart about a 1964 case concerned with defining obscenity, "I know it when I see it".

Perhaps the American writer Frank Gruber did the best job of summarising the genre when he identified seven basic plots for Westerns:

Union Pacific story: The plot concerns construction of a railroad, a telegraph line or some other type of modern technology on the wild frontier. Wagon-train stories fall into this category.

Ranch story: Ranchers protecting their family ranch from rustlers or large landowners attempting to force out the proper owners.

Empire story: The plot involves building a ranch empire or an oil empire from scratch, a classic rags-to-riches plot, often involving conflict over resources such as water or minerals.

Revenge story: The plot often involves an elaborate chase and pursuit by a wronged individual, but it may also include elements of the classic mystery story.

Cavalry and Indian story: The plot revolves around "taming" the wilderness for white settlers and/or fighting Native Americans.

Outlaw story: The outlaw gangs dominate the action.

Marshal story: The lawman and his challenges drive the plot.

Most films in the genre fall into one of these seven stories but not all as we shall see. Some of the greatest Westerns fall into several categories and sometimes are so innovative as to create their own. The timeframe is important too and ranges only over fifty years, from 1849 to 1899. This is an incredibly short period of history. It is also worth noting that while the Wild West had many books written about it, America itself was a global backwater. This period coincides with the Victorian Era in Britain, the pinnacle of the British Empire, but France, Russia and Germany were no slouches at colonisation either. Cowboys may have been cool, but they weren't historically relevant in an era that lasted less than a human lifetime. It turns out that being a cowboy was not a career that was passed down the generations.

It is an entirely unintuitive fact that the first dramatic reconstruction of the Wild West on film was not made in America, but Blackburn, England. *Kidnapping by Indians* is from 1899 and was made by the Mitchell and Kenyon film company. It was a novelty moving picture and would have been shown at fairs or vaudeville shows. It is all of two minutes long, so calling it a narrative film is going too far, but the plot is familiar to anyone who has watched a few Westerns. Native Americans (the "Indians" of the title, all played by Englishmen) attack a white settlers' camp, set it on fire and kidnap a girl. However, just before they head off with their ill-gotten gains, a posse of cowboys arrives, a gunfight ensues, and the captured girl is rescued by the cowboys. They packed a lot into a couple of minutes, but despite the racism and the cultural appropriation, this 1899 film created a blueprint for dozens of American-made Westerns for the next sixty years. While *Kidnapping by Indians* came first, it is highly unlikely that it was seen in America and therefore is more a point of novelty rather than anything to do with the foundations of the American film industry.

Now let's debunk the most common trope in all of Hollywood: cowboys never fought natives in extended gun battles. Just a cursory glance at the history of the western frontier makes it clear this couldn't have happened. All this land had previously been native territory; the settlers didn't clear the land, the US Army did. By the time the settlers were establishing farms and later ranches full of cattle, the native populations had been denuded by war, famine and disease and were living largely on reservations.

One of the first motion pictures considered to be a narrative movie from America is the eleven/twelve-minute-long *The Great Train Robbery* from 1903 (nearly a decade before the term Western seems to have been used, and more than five times longer than *Kidnapping by Indians*). In the film bandits hold up a train and are subsequently chased by a brave posse. This was not only the first Western, but this was also one of the first-ever narrative movie. It's silent, it's black and white, and it's about as long as half an episode of *Friends*. And yet from these humble beginnings an entire industry was born.

To show how close to the birth of moving pictures this was, the exact length of the film is up for debate. It is twelve minutes long if it is run at eighteen frames a second. The cameras at the time were hand-cranked, so to maintain a fluid shutter speed with the movement of the cameraman, eighteen frames per second were recorded. Today the standard is twenty-four. This means that some prints of early black and white footage appear to run fast because they are run at twenty-four. With modern computers and various AI programmes, the missing frames on some early films have been added in. Perhaps the most impressive example of this is the Peter Jackson-directed documentary about World War I from 2018, *They Shall Not Grow Old*. In that case the frame rate has been upped to twenty-four, the footage meticulously colourised and sound added (including the regional accents of the regiments) to bring to life a century-old conflict.

At the end of 1990's *Goodfellas*, Joe Pesci, a character I had watched die earlier in the film, turns up in the last scene. He stands emotionless, staring out at the audience, a revolver in his right hand; he fires all six shots directly at the viewer. The first time I saw this, I had no idea why the scene was there, and narratively, it made no sense. What I now know is that this was Martin Scorsese showing us that he had done his homework while also making the point that not only has crime always been a part of human society, but also that it has always been a draw for moviegoers. I later discovered that this scene in *Goodfellas* was a deliberate and direct reference to *The Great Train Robbery*, a film released eighty-seven years earlier.

The Great Train Robbery was made by Edwin S Porter (the film's release date means it's a little too early to use the term "director"). The film pre-dates all the major movie studios, so this was made for the Edison Manufacturing Company (yes, that Edison). In the film we saw a ten-gallon hat wearing, moustachioed bank robber carry out the scene described in *Goodfellas*. We are at such a stage of infancy in the industry that this separate piece of footage was sent out by the Edison Manufacturing Company informing projectionists that they could run the scene either at the front or at the end of the film. Today it is always run at the end (which is why it's at the end of *Goodfellas*). The film provided the blueprint for the perfect Western; there are good guys chasing bad guys, there are exciting scenes on a locomotive, there are shootouts and riders on horses dashing across the screen, everything the paying public would expect from a Western fifty or a hundred years later.

The motifs of the Western have been so indelibly etched into our subconscious that a black and white silent movie doesn't seem like the correct medium for a Western. The irony of this is all the primary source materials from the second half of the 19th century are black and white and silent. But as we shall later see, the reality of frontier life will frequently be discordant with the cinematic version.

The Great Train Robbery wasn't filmed anywhere near the great frontiers. Instead, it was shot in New York and New Jersey, states about as far to the east as you can get in America (but admittedly, closer than Blackburn). The film continues to stir quite the academic debate: to some it has become mythologised and deserves its place in the Library of Congress. To others it is overrated as they point out that it wasn't the first narrative movie (I was careful about the phrasing above), and that narratively, it was a dead end, having nothing of real interest to say. But the use of close ups, location shooting and some action (others might call it violence) meant that it was wildly successful. It might not have been the first narrative motion picture, but it was the first blockbuster. People went to see it more than once, and the crowds gathering to see the next showing indicated that people had told their friends. Reviews didn't exist in those days, but the age-old phrase "you can't track enthusiasm" could have been coined for this film. It's called show business for a reason, and *The Great Train Robbery* was great business every time it showed.

While *The Great Train Robbery* is not the most beloved or even the most competently directed Western, it was the starting point. Other silent movies in this chapter came out a decade or more after this film, that's how ahead of its time it was. Indeed, it's worth remembering that this film came out during Butch Cassidy and the Sundance Kid's real escapades. Wyatt Earp and Buffalo Bill were still very much alive. While no attempt at historical accuracy or any recreation of specific events was ever intended, they couldn't get the props and clothing wrong because the film was contemporary to the times.

It is also worth noting that the film is the first story to present the planning, execution and then results of a robbery, therefore technically making it the first heist movie. While the DNA of the heist film with the gathering of the team and the explanation of the plan wasn't to be perfected until the 1950s in the likes of *The Killing* or *Rififi*. The start of this crime subgenre starts with a western. Films like *Heat*, *Ocean's 11* and even *The Dark Knight* owe it a debt of gratitude.

Then something that had nothing to do with the Wild West would change Hollywood forever: World War I. The beauty of silent movies is they can be made in any country and then, provided the written plates are translated into the local language, they can be shown globally. France, Germany and Britain all had thriving film sectors, and it is worth remembering that at the time of *The Great Train Robbery*, America was a junior partner on the global stage. At the time Britain had the world's largest empire. As such, while American movies were popular, they were only one of the many countries making films in the first decade of the 20th century. However, with the outbreak of war in 1914, the European powers had better things to do than make movies. The young men in these countries were needed for the armies, and millions would die or be wounded. While America joined the fighting in 1917, the impact on America was minimal compared to the losses suffered by Germany, Russia and France. So, while Europe was in flames, America got on with the entertainment business. California had the edge over the East Coast due to its weather. Early cameras needed a lot of light and while many scenes in the early Hollywood films may appear to be indoors, they were often filmed out in the open. Free lighting plus the varied locations of mountains, forests, deserts and the coast nearby meant most stories could be filmed with the minimum of cost. In short, Hollywood was lucky due to geography, weather and the lack of war.

Just before the outbreak of war in 1913, there was another important Western, *The Battle of Elderbush Gulch,* directed by D W Griffith. Griffith is important in the history of narrative film making; his editing and scale of storytelling makes him the uncle of the Hollywood epic - albeit the racist uncle. His 1915 movie *Birth of a Nation* is incredibly important in the technical creation of feature films - one version runs for over three hours - but it is shockingly racist, its politics were controversial even in 1915. The story of how the Ku Klux Klan "saved" the South from evil northerners and Black people is not historically accurate. So, while it's an important part of the story of cinema, it is toxic in its views and depictions of race in the modern world.

You could say what *Birth of a Nation* did for white/black relations, *The Battle of Elderbush Gulch* did for white and native relations. The promotional poster shows a native warrior about to toss a white child to the ground. Sadly, racism will rear its ugly head a few more times in this book, but while some racism occurs through ignorance, Griffiths seems to deploy it with a streak of genuine malice. The film itself centres on white settlers being surrounded by native peoples. The term "Cowboys and Indians" is now redundant and is regarded as casually racist, but for generations of children around the world (me included), this was a popular playground game. It was an ignorant version of good guys versus bad guys, and while *The Battle of Elderbush Gulch* did not invent the game, the adult version is here writ large on the screen. Griffith was a racist, but he was also one of the greatest directors of the age. The shootouts, the galloping horses, the near misses and last-gasp saves are well done even by modern standards. The film lasts around twenty-nine minutes and packs a lot into its brief running time, but there can be no doubt that it's the white men who are the good guys, and the natives are one-dimensional bad guys. The film is an expertly shot and directed game of "Cowboys and Indians". When I played it, I was six years old and lived in England. Griffiths doesn't have an excuse.

Then there's *The Three Godfathers*. This is the classic situation of tough men being made vulnerable by a child. It's based on a 1913 novel by Peter B Kyne. In the novel, one of four bank robbers dies as the gang escapes the scene of the crime, but the movie opens after the bank robbery and focusses on the three outlaws as they flee a pursuing posse. Travelling through the desert they find a dying woman and her baby in a wagon; she makes the men promise to take care of her baby and get it to safety. This allows the filmmakers to give us sweeping vistas of harsh desert scenery while a perennially tense chase plays out. The men must keep moving, and yet even these hardened outlaws feel protective of this innocent new life for which they are now responsible. The film stars Harry Carey, and he thought the story was such a good idea that he made it again three years later in 1919 as *Marked Men*. This time the film was directed by John Ford who, in 1948, would go back and make it yet again, this time changing the name back to *The Three Godfathers*. By then Carey was dead, but Ford dedicated the movie to him as a mark of respect.

Why did this particular novel get three movie versions? Because these films made money. All the silent Westerns did was replace the dime novel and Buffalo Bill's Wild West Show with an easy-t0-consume piece of escapism. They were cheap to make and far cheaper to distribute than the cumbersome wagon train of a live Wild West show. The whole idea of these films was that they had no point of reference in the real world for the majority of viewers, whether urban Americans or farmers in Italy. The movie industry was escapism on an industrial level, and the whole world wanted some of the excitement of the Wild Frontier.

In the middle of all of this was a young man in his early twenties called John Feeney. Early on he took the directorial name of Jack Ford but didn't think that was quite right and finally settled on John Ford. He got into the industry via his brother who was twelve years his senior, but by 1917 he had begun directing shorts (of his sixty silent films over the next eleven years, only ten remain which are complete or near complete). Although Ford would go on to become one of the directors whose career was synonymous with Westerns, a closer look at his filmography reveals far more variety, and a number of his other films will appear in this book. But let's start with his first feature film (there are still extant copies), 1917's *Straight Shooting*. Ford directed this when he was only twenty-three.

The film stars Harry Carey, a perfect example of Hollywood typecasting from as far back as 1917. He was from New York, but because of Montana, a Western play he wrote and starred in, he became associated with cowboy roles. People accepted he was an overall good actor, but he drew his biggest crowds when he was playing a cowboy. Carey was a star ... provided he stuck to Westerns. So, we now have a new director and a bankable star, with a movie in the genre that was guaranteed to get the moviegoers in. Once again, we see the Hollywood of a century ago echoing through the decades to the Hollywood of today. Nobody wants to risk a flop and moviegoers are fickle. A well-known actor in a well-known story mitigated the risk of a twenty-three-year-old behind the camera.

Straight Shooting is an incredibly impressive (full) directorial debut. What is on display is a clear evolution from the time of *The Great Train Robbery,* including the wide-angle shots that Ford would come to be associated with in the era of colour and sound. The scope is wider, the camera more confident. As Harry walks away, his back to the camera, Winchester in hand, aiming at the bad guy, it could be a shot from a Leone spaghetti Western. The tag line has a timeless ring to it: "A story of a western bad man who turned to the right through the influence of a haunting pair of hazel eyes". How many mid-century Westerns could be that succinctly summed up? The stunts are genuinely thrilling, and we see in one sixty-two-minute film the exhilaration of the genre and the directorial flair of a future great.

While it was prescient in many aspects, it was also a film of its time. The interior of the cabin is strangely bright, and as the tablecloth seems to be moving in the wind, it's a reminder that this was neither shot on location nor in a studio, but outside, using the bright Californian sun (and directional reflectors) to light the scene.

Ford only improved. In 1924 he made *The Iron Horse* (the name is the Native American term for a steam locomotive), considered to be his first major work and telling the story of the construction of America's transcontinental railway. Native Americans, Chinese and Irish are all depicted here. This is not a whitewashing of American history, rather a genuine portrayal of the minority labour force that made the dream a reality. Equally importantly, this is the first time the First Nation people are not portrayed as the villains. The bad guy is a corrupt businessman who pretends to be a renegade Cheyenne. As such it is surprisingly woke for a film of the 1920s: the bad guy is white, the innocent bystanders are hardworking minorities, but the good guys are, of course, also white guys.

The film is also notable as one of the first Westerns to become novelised. The publisher Grosset and Dunlap had won the rights to novelise multiple studio films. This was a way of earning more money from a movie and a practice that would last into the early 21st century. Before widely available home entertainment, the way to relive the film you enjoyed was to buy the book. Long before the idea of continuity and "cannon lore" writers would add extra scenes and internal monologues to provide new interpretations of the movies. The film did not have to be a literary drama, but it could be a very visual kinetic experience. Personally, I remember pouring over the novelisations of *The Empire Strikes Back*, *Rocky IV* and *Mad Max Beyond Thunderdome*, none of which would immediately be thought of as movies that could be books, but they were. In the age of silent movies, a novelisation made even more sense as there were only so many storyboards people would be willing to read, so in the case of *The Iron Horse*, the novel acted as a companion piece, enlarging and enriching the film version.

Even in the 1920s people knew how to promote. The ceremony linking both ends of the transcontinental railway took place in the Utah Territory in 1869, with a golden spike to celebrate the final connection. This was a huge moment for America, and the ceremony where the two steam engines faced each other is reenacted in the film with the claim that both original engines had been used in the making of the movie. This was, to be polite, not accurate because both trains had been decommissioned years earlier and different locomotives were used. But Hollywood has never let facts get in the way of a good story. However, the ultimate silent film about locomotives came out two years later in 1926, with Buster Keaton's *The General*. Because the film is set during the US Civil War (which is era appropriate, with a variety of Westerns being intertwined with the Civil War) this technically falls into the war movie genre, but it is such a stone-cold classic Western it must be added in this chapter. Besides explosions, chases and stunts on a train it has many of the same elements of many Westerns, *The Great Train Robbery* in particular. This screenplay was written by Keaton, and the film was co-directed by him and starred him. It was his masterpiece and is loosely (very loosely) based on some real history so unbelievable that it is worth pausing to recount this true civil war story.

The Andrew's Raid, sometimes known as the Great Locomotive Chase was a Union (the North) raid deep into Confederate (the South) territory. It occurred in 1862 when volunteers from the Union army, led by a civilian scout called James Andrews, commandeered a train called The General and drove it along the Western and Atlantic Railroad, intent on causing as much damage as possible. The Union forces cut the telegraph lines so Confederate forces along the route had no idea what was coming. Once the raid was in progress, the Confederates chased on foot, on horse and later, on trains for over eighty-seven miles. The disruption was huge, but the Union soldiers were eventually captured. A number were summarily executed as spies. It's worth noting that Keaton was so eager to link his passion project to real events that the titular locomotive of the film was the name of the train in the real raid. It was a highly effective raid with a grim ending and not the obvious topic for a comedy.

In the film Keaton plays Johnnie Gray, a southerner but also not exactly enthusiastic follower of the secessionist cause. Because his work as a locomotive engineer is vital to the war effort, he can't enlist in the army, so he continues to drive The General, a job he had taken mainly to impress a girl. True to history, Andrews turns up, and he and his raiders take over The General while Johnny is off duty. The problem is that the girl he wants to impress is on the train. So, Johnnie (like the Confederacy in real life) chases after the train, first on foot, then on a bike and later, on a hand car. Eventually, he manages to get on the train. It is at this point the film goes from amazing to perfection. The number of gags Keaton uses with a real locomotive are simply stunning, for instance, sitting on the piston rod as if it were a chair and watching it slowly rotate him as the wheels of the train roll along. And then there's the famous scene where Keaton, positioned on the cow-catcher, throws a wooden sleeper at a loose sleeper on the rails to bounce it out of the way before it can derail the locomotive. Of course, all this was done decades before CGI, and he did the stunts for real.

A lot of moviegoers today are not interested in silent movies. The view is they lack ambition, subtlety, even technical competence. Like any artform in its infancy, many things were later improved, but silent story telling could at times be as subtle or exhilarating as any modern blockbuster. Serious skills and effort were put into the production of *The General*. In the spring of 1926, the film's location manager, Burt Jackson, found an area in Oregon with old-fashioned railroads, perfect for the civil war setting. Jackson also discovered that in the same area, the Pacific and Eastern Railway owned two period-appropriate locomotives, so he bought them. He later bought a third locomotive for the biggest set piece, a train falling into a river when the bridge is demolished beneath it. It is a shot that is still impressive to this day because it was done for real.

The cast and crew arrived on location in Oregon with eighteen freight cars full of civil war-era cannons, rebuilt passenger cars, stagecoaches, houses, wagons and, of course, workers to build everything. The effort to create Keaton's vision was huge. At this time Keaton had complete control over his film projects, but in his quest to get everything just right on this technically challenging shoot, the budget ballooned from $400,000 to $750,000, over $13 million in today's money and a colossal amount for the time. A film this ambitious, using multiple locomotives meant that, inevitably, there would be accidents. Keaton was knocked unconscious in one scene, but far more worryingly, an assistant director was accidentally shot in the face with a blank. One of the locomotive's wheels ran over a brakeman's foot, resulting in a lawsuit costing the production thousands. Further, there were many problems with the wood-burning engines which caused numerous fires that sometimes spread to nearby forests and farmers' haystacks. The locals knew the production had money and charged them a then whopping $25 per burnt stack.

Calling this movie Keaton's obsession is not an exaggeration; he poured his heart and soul into it. *The General* came out to mixed reviews and was met with a lukewarm box office. It wasn't a flop, but it was far more expensive to make than the studio had intended, and the returns didn't cover the inflated budget, let alone make a profit. This was the last time Keaton was in complete control of his work; after this, the studios had him on a short leash. With hindsight, the film was probably too ambitious for moviegoers at that time. But whatever the reasons for the reluctance of the general public at the time of the original release, this black and white silent film got a new lease of life in 1954. Someone failed to renew the copyright registration, so the film passed into the public domain. This meant that TV channels had a ready seventy-eight-minute film that could be used for free, so *The General* could now be accessed by a whole new generation and, as a result, had far greater exposure compared to other silent films (it was the same story with *It's a Wonderful Life*).

Some critics pointed out (not unfairly) that it's hard to get a laugh out of war, except this film absolutely did and does an amazing balancing act of showing respect for the bravery of soldiers while never lionising the South and still being laugh-out-loud funny. Failure to renew the copyright meant the film had a longer life than anyone could have anticipated, and it influenced a new generation of filmmakers. The artistry was there for all to see. It became a film deemed so important that it has been preserved in the Library of Congress for being "culturally, historically, or aesthetically significant".

The star of *The Iron Horse* was Harry Carey, a bankable star if he was in a Western, but the true giant of the silent Western genre was Thomas Hezikiah Mix, known by his star name as simply Tom Mix. Mix was born in 1880 in Mix Run, Pennsylvania. While he did learn to ride as a boy, Pennsylvania is a long way from the Wild Frontier. He joined the army at eighteen when the Spanish-American War broke out, but his unit was never posted overseas, so he saw no action. Apparently, army life was not for him because after one furlough he never returned. He married in 1902 and liked that so much he went on to marry a total of five times. As a star, exaggerated rumours swirled about his military service. I have read that he served with American forces at the time of the Boxer Rebellion in China, but there is no evidence for this. He himself said he fought in the Second Boer War, and again, there is no evidence. But the idea of a man willing to fight for his country in exotic, overseas locations lent a certain cachet.

In 1909, Mix had his screen debut in a short film called *The Cowboy Millionaire*. A year later things really changed when he appeared as himself in a short documentary film, *Ranch Life in the Great Southwest*. His years of working in stables meant he could show off his ranching skills, and he became the epitome of the onscreen cowboy. From this point on he never looked back. Between 1909 and 1935, he appeared in 291 films, all but nine of which were silent films. This shows you the sheer volume of movies being produced in America. If he had reached a total of 312 it would have meant he had made a movie for every month of his career.

Mix liked things simple. He always played the hero (naturally) and almost always wore a pure white ten-gallon hat. White hats and black hats are terms that have seeped into many different sectors, but they originated in the Western when the hero in the early days invariably wore a light-coloured hat while the bad guy usually wore a black (or dark brown) one. Before the era of sound or colour, such simple visual cues were needed to help the audience follow what was going on.

Mix was fearless. He did his own stunts, and sometimes, off set, he conducted shows to prove that he was the real deal (this included bull riding). In the 1920s, he bought a ranch in Arizona and had it converted into a frontier town, with areas that simulated desert so that now he had everything he needed to tell his next story. This permanent set, this frontier town was dubbed Mixville. By now Mix was commanding a salary of $7,500 a week, a huge sum for the times; he was so famous that his trusty ride Tony became known as Tony the Wonder Horse and was a celebrity in his own right. In fact, Tony was so famous that he had his own subgenre of stories known as the "Wonder Horse" stories. Champion was the name given to a series of horses who had films and even TV shows made about them. They were called *Champion the Wonder Horse* and I watched the reruns as a kid.

So, what about budgets. The grander Westerns, with sweeping narratives spread over decades and a cast of hundreds had very large budgets for the time, but the reason Hollywood loved them was because they were cheap to make, something that Tom Mix virtually industrialised. Let's imagine you want to make your first movie, but movies are, on the whole, expensive to make. You will have trouble getting funding because you're untested and won't attract big name stars because you are unknown in the industry; potential backers have no idea if people will turn out to see your work. So, with a tiny budget you have to pick a film genre that you know people will want to see. In the first half of the 20th century that meant Westerns. In the 1990s, it meant crime films; *El Mariachi*, *Reservoir Dogs* and *Lock Stock and Two Smoking Barrels* were all debut films of then unknown directors who would go on to have successful careers. All three of these movies were filmed for peanuts but brought in ten or twenty times that at the box office alone. In the 21st century, that genre is horror. A low-budget film on a topic people can't get enough of means not many people have to see it to turn a profit. 2023's *Fast X* had a production budget of $340 million, which meant that the film had to be approaching a billion dollars at the box office just to break even. People like Tom Mix knew that the main cost of a Western is the sets and the horses. If you already have them, the production costs are substantially smaller. The great outdoors looks impressive onscreen and it's free. Tom Mix was a savvy businessman who arranged things so that he was the most expensive commodity on the set.

By 1929, Mix's salary had ballooned to $20,000 a week, but this was the year tragedy struck. Mix had become friends with Wyatt Earp, and when Earp died, a screen legend was the pallbearer for a real legend. Then there was the stock market crash and Mix's fourth divorce. He wasn't broke, but in today's money he had amassed a fortune worth over $126 million, which was now largely wiped out. A third blow came with the rise of talking motion pictures, at which point Mix realised that for him the game was over. He had put himself in harm's way multiple times while filming his hundreds of movies, and after numerous breaks of his nose and damage to his throat after having been accidentally shot, he just didn't have the voice for the era of sound. He continued to work, performing stunts in the circus, and from the 1930s into the 1950s he leant his name to the hugely popular radio show *Tom Mix Ralston Straight Shooters*. It never featured his voice, but his image was used in the promotional material and the royalties kept him comfortable.

Mix never heard the last performance of the radio show as he died in a car accident in 1940, but Tony the Wonder Horse outlived his owner. The Tom Mix story is an interesting one and tells us something about the fleeting nature of celebrity. In 1925, you could have asked any moviegoer in the world if they had heard of Tom Mix, and they would all have enthusiastically replied, yes, and yet today, he is completely unknown. My father, born and raised in a small town in the Republic of Türkiye remembers devouring Tom Mix comic books in the 1950s, and that's how I first heard of him.

As a man, Mix was far from perfect. He cut his daughter out of his will when she couldn't keep his circus open while he was in Europe, and then there were the multiple marriages. He was described by the studio head of FBO Pictures as a "tight-assed, money-crazy son of a bitch". But this assessment would begin to sound familiar over the coming years when other actors behaved badly. While keeping things together professionally, lives off set were often in chaos. But Mix had a soft side too. He never expected someone to do a stunt he couldn't do himself and regularly got hurt doing his own stunts; he was Jackie Chan fifty years before Jackie Chan. He was friends with many other celebrities and introduced studio workers to people like Wyatt Earp. That was certainly the powerful memory of a young college dropout called Marion Morrison, who would later change his name to John Wayne. Is it any wonder that Wayne fashioned his cowboy character of an impeccably good man who wore a big hat after his hero Tom Mix? But Mix, too, had another name, often used by the next generation of Hollywood actors who took on roles in Westerns, "King of the Cowboys".

Chapter 2

The Distant Sound of Gunfire

Al Jolson's *The Jazz Singer* came out in 1927. There had been a few experiments with the "talkies" before this, but this was the first major release by a major studio, and it was a major hit. With this one film the musical genre was born and created a major headache for distributors. While movie theatres existed at the time, silent movies could be played anywhere because all you needed was a projector and a white sheet. In many small communities, films were shown in church halls, the one area that could seat a crowd of several hundred. This arrangement generated revenue for the church and allowed the local clergyman to assess the film for its suitability (this little piece of cinematic history is marvellously recreated in *Cinema Paradiso* where the priest watches the new films and rings a bell every time he wants something edited out). But the talkies were about to change all this as what local church had the money for audio equipment?

To the modern generation a black and white film is a hard sell. The world is in colour so there is already a layer of artifice when it becomes monochromatic, and any attempt to entertain with silent motion pictures is an impossibility with audiences today. The shortcomings of a silent film are especially obvious in Westerns. People might think that Technicolor is needed to bring a cowboy movie to life, but in reality it is its sound. No amount of crashing cymbals or staccato drumming can replace that sharp, violent, percussive explosion that is gunfire. Watching a silent shootout feels more wrong than watching a black and white one. Jolson may have taught Hollywood how to sing, but he also opened the gates for so many creative choices for the Western that the genre took this new technology and made it its own.

Before going any further it should be noted that the lives of most cowboys as depicted in Western movies are not realistic; the job of a cowboy was cattle herding, and there is very little of that in most of these films. The roles most usually portrayed are those of a sheriff (or other law enforcement), bounty hunter, robber, gambler, bandit, prospector, tracker, soldier, ranch hand and gun-for-hire. All these existed and sometimes people did more than one in a lifetime, but according to Hollywood, the era of the cowboy, which in reality lasted perhaps twenty years from post-civil war America to the late 1880s, defined America's West from around 1865-1900.

Sound created huge disruptions for Hollywood. It put an end to the careers of the great silent comedians Chaplin and Keaton. They would have a few final hurrahs, but their glory days were behind them. A huge swathe of Hollywood royalty was dethroned as they had been cast for their looks and not their acting ability. British actors, honed on the stage where speech, nuance and live acting were in the job description, were shipped in. It also helped that they were cheaper than established Hollywood names. Tom Mix's monumental career came to an end simply because he didn't sound very good, but he was not the only one.

In 1931, RKO Pictures released *Cimarron*. Starring Richard Dix and Irene Dunne, the poster proudly declared "Terrific as all Creation" (Hollywood never had a problem with hyperbole). It was directed by Wesley Ruggles, a man who had been directing movies since 1917. He was never one of the greats, but he was a safe pair of hands. The film was epic in scope, spanning forty years from 1889 to 1929, and epic in budget, costing around $1.5 million to make. The story is set around a newspaper editor who is looking for some adventure and in 1889 settles in an Oklahoma boom town with his reluctant wife; various scrapes and escapades ensue as they try to build a new life together. And for the first time in this book, we can talk about dialogue. In *Cimarron* there is an exchange between husband and wife showing the gruff pragmatism that not only defines the Western hero, but also many noir and antiheroes of the future:

"Did you have to kill him like that?"
"No, I could have let him kill me."

With this one film we get the strengths and the weaknesses of the Western distilled. The point of the film was to entertain and make money (although it failed to achieve that in its initial release). There is not a bad or cynical bone in its body. Like many Westerns this is a romp: you pay your money, watch the film, eat your popcorn and come out quoting lines and seeing who draws the fastest pretend gun. But for all of that, it was hanging a supposedly carefree story on some brutally harsh realities.

Frank Gruber was a prolific writer of pulp fiction Westerns, and *Cimarron* breaks his list of plots for Western stories. The film isn't about an outlaw or anyone looking for revenge, and while the lead does set up his own newspaper, he's hardly trying to build an empire. Also, half the film's timeline lies outside of Gruber's timeframe. All this shows how hard it is to define the Western genre. This is emphasised by the fact that this movie, towards the end, overlaps in time with *Killers of the Flower Moon*, which has already been mentioned as a film that could be a Western, but nobody thinks it is. In that movie a huge amount of time and attention are spent on the plight and deaths of the Osage people. In *Cimarron* they are just background or part of a vague stage setting, and yet this was filmed around the time the murders were actually taking place in Osage County. Director Ruggles did not intentionally make *Cimarron* culturally insensitive, but if you watch *Killers of the Flower Moon* first, you can't watch *Cimarron* and not be aware of its rose-tinted glasses.

Unfortunately, it gets worse. The trigger for the *Cimarron* hero to head west was the very real Oklahoma Land Rush, which started at high noon (when else?) on 22 April 1889. An estimated 50,000 people were lined up at the start, all seeking to gain a piece of the available two million acres. Native peoples were exempt from the process. This was the first land run into the unassigned lands of former Indian Territory, which had earlier been assigned to the Muscogee and Seminole peoples. The story of the western advance of the American nation across the continent (the original thirteen colonies were all on the East Coast) is one of complete disregard for the native populations to the point that their very existence was endangered. As the white settlers moved west, the natives fought back, but having been annihilated by European diseases such as smallpox, and then fighting against vastly technologically superior soldiers meant that they were fighting a losing war of survival. Therefore, many native people ended up surrendering to the federal government which then moved them into designated areas (rarely their homeland). However, as the land grabs became more flagrant many native peoples were moved again and again onto ever poorer land. In the year 1500, the population of North America was 100% native peoples; by 2000, it was 1%. At best this was ethnic cleansing, at worse it was genocide. Today there are American politicians who claim that America has never gone to war over land, except for the space to bury their dead. This was largely true in the 20th century, but how did America grow from thirteen states to fifty if not by taking land from the native populations?

The Osage people are arguably the most cursed in history. Having faced multiple existential threats, eventually being settled on land too poor for farming but then discovering oil beneath their feet sounds like a story that might have a happy ending. But that was not to be as the riches promised by oil made them the target for new threats and unleashed the predators who would do anything (including committing murder) to get their hands on the Osage lands. NONE of this is mentioned in *Cimarron*. The movie was based on a novel of the same name by Edna Ferber which came out just a year earlier, and there was a bit of diversity around the film. It was made in the depths of the Great Depression (as were all the movies in the 30s), but the scale was huge despite the economic climate. The land rush scene was recreated with 5,000 extras and had twenty-eight cameras filming the action, resulting in a sight that would dazzle even the modern moviegoer. While set in Oklahoma, the whole film was shot in California (naturally). Art director Max Ree obviously knew how Tom Mix made his movies because he was able to get RKO to buy eighty-nine acres where he built a whole frontier town. This was important because after shooting, RKO didn't pull it down but instead, continued to use it and add to it, making it their very own Mixville. Once again we see the economy of Westerns.

While *Cimarron* the film was not initially a big earner, the money that had been spent on the sets turned out to be a real money spinner for RKO. One frontier town looked much like all the others (in reality they didn't, but they do in the movies), so the clapboard houses, the general store and the legendary swinging doors to the town saloon became iconic signifiers that the audience was in the Wild West as other movie studios paid to shoot their latest Western on the *Cimarron* set - better than spending money to build your own.

Even though *Cimarron* was not initially profitable the critics raved about it. Westerns were generally looked down upon as one of the lower forms of the cinema world, rather like superhero or action movies in the 21st century. It is true that some are just bad, but then there are the great films in any genre. While *Cimarron* was always meant to entertain, the fact that it was adapted from a novel meant it had aspirations beyond the average Tom Mix movie. As such, it won a number of Academy Awards (everyone calls them the Oscars so I will be using that term moving forwards), including Outstanding Production, which is now Best Picture, the first Western to do so. It would take more than fifty years for another Western to win one.

This tension between popular but low art can be shown by Marlon Brando who is undoubtedly one of the greatest actors of all time - he only ever directed one movie and that was *One-Eyed Jacks*. This 1961 Western received critically mixed reviews at the time but is now considered to be a great Western, a film that feels like a bridge between the classic John Wayne Westerns and the grittier, earthier Spaghetti Westerns. And films considered to be classics today, such as *The Good, the Bad and the Ugly* weren't even nominated for any Oscars. They were seen as too vulgar.

However, once the Oscars were over, *Cimarron* was re-released and made its money back. This is worth exploring a little more. The way the Oscars worked for more than seventy years was that the so-called "better" films of the year were the ones nominated. More effort may have been put into them, but also, they were popular. *Gone With the Wind*, *West Side Story*, *The Godfather* and *Titanic* were all at some point the biggest grossing movie of all time, and they were also showered with golden statues. These were clearly the movies that people wanted to see, so once the Oscars brought *Cimarron* back to public attention in the midst of the Great Depression, moviegoers spent their incredibly precious thirty-five cents (the average cost of a movie ticket in 1931) to see the film everyone was talking about. Now fast forward to the 2020s, and in today's film industry there are popular movies like *A Minecraft Movie*, which is never going to be considered for an Oscar but cleans up at the box office. Or how about *CODA*, a fine small film about deaf parents with a hearing daughter and their small-town life; it didn't excite the global box office, but it won the Oscar for Best Picture. A great case study around this occurred in 2020 (Covid changed everything) when we had *Nomadland*, written and directed by Chloé Zhao and starring Frances McDormand. This very modest film is about the life of a modern nomad, a woman who chooses to sell her home and live in a van. The movie cost only $5 million to make and internationally grossed just under $40 million, so it more than covered its costs, but has that plot summary made you want to watch it? There's a scene where we see the reality of taking a dump in a bucket in the back of a van. I am not making this up. The academy is trying to make the Oscars relevant to the TikTok generation, and while Westerns aren't necessarily the solution, back in 1931, the studios knew what movies audiences wanted – and made them. Today in Hollywood most of the big box office movies aren't aimed at winning awards, and the films regarded as Oscar-worthy are so niche nobody goes to see them. Fortunately, with movies like *Oppenheimer* we can see that Hollywood has not forgotten how to make more mature movies that can garner awards and still kill it at the box office.

While *Cimarron* is more about a journalist than a gunslinger there are still plenty of gun shots, and of course, now we get the brutal crack of gunfire rather than just the puff of smoke seen in silent films. Sound makes the fights more immediate - more violent. The film was remade in 1960 in colour, and the name *Cimarron* has been used for numerous lesser Westerns, including that rarest of things, an animated Western, specifically the 2002 Dreamworks' animated movie called *Spirit: Stallion of the Cimarron* (Matt Damon voices the horse).

Another way to describe *Cimarron* was that it was a "pre-code" movie. My references to gun shots and violence are deliberate because now, with sound, every movie was more intense. How much violence could be shown? Was swearing allowed? The use of sound had unleashed something new, and it quickly became clear that content needed to be regulated. In 1929, a silent film from France called *Un Chien Andalou* was directed by Luis Buñuel, with a screenplay by Salvador Dalí. With images of a razor blade about to cut through the eye of a woman and a closeup of the blade cutting through the eyeball of a cow, the film shocked anyone who watched it. It makes for uncomfortable viewing even in the 21st century, and while *Un Chien Andalou* was an art house movie that was never going to reach the mainstream, the medium of cinema was getting more and more debauched every year.

So, to counter this rise in sex, violence and swearing, the Motion Picture Production Code was introduced as a set of self-regulatory guidelines for content released by major studios in America from 1934 to 1968. It was more commonly known as the Hays Code, after Will H Hays, president of the Motion Picture Producers and Distributors of America at the time of creation. It was taken from an earlier 1927 recommendation and the list is worth republishing in full as it's a wonderful snapshot of the main moral concerns at the time, with the result that films should not contain or portray:

> Pointed profanity—by either title or lip—this includes the words God, Lord, Jesus, Christ (unless they be used reverently in connection

with proper religious ceremonies), Hell, S.O.B., damn, Gawd, and every other profane and vulgar expression however it may be spelled.

Any licentious or suggestive nudity—in fact or in silhouette; and any lecherous or licentious notice thereof by other characters in the picture

The illegal traffic in drugs
Any inference of sex perversion (that meant homosexuality)
White slavery
Miscegenation
Sex hygiene and venereal diseases
Scenes of actual childbirth—in fact or in silhouette
Children's sex organs
Ridicule of the clergy
Wilful offense to any nation, race or creed (this one was broken regularly);
and
BE IT FURTHER RESOLVED (their capitals, not mine), that special care be exercised in the manner in which the following subjects are treated, to the end that vulgarity and suggestiveness may be eliminated and that good taste may be emphasized:

The use of the Flag
International Relations (avoid picturizing in an unfavorable light another country's religion, history, institutions, prominent people and citizenry)
Arson
The use of firearms
Theft, robbery, safe-cracking, and dynamiting of trains, mines, buildings, et cetera (having in mind the effect which a too-detailed description of these may have upon the moron)
Brutality and possible gruesomeness

Technique of committing murder by whatever method
Methods of smuggling
Third-Degree methods
Actual hangings or electrocutions as legal punishment for crime
Sympathy for criminals
Attitude toward public characters and institutions
Sedition
Apparent cruelty to children and animals
Branding of people or animals
The sale of women, or of a woman selling her virtue
Rape or attempted rape
First-night scenes
Man and woman in bed together
Deliberate seduction of girls
The institution of marriage
Surgical operations
The use of drugs
Titles or scenes having to do with law enforcement or law-enforcing officers
Excessive or lustful kissing, particularly when one character or the other is a "heavy"

It's quite a list, and even relatively innocent films made from 1969 onwards would fail at the code. Further, defining "lustful kissing" meant no on-screen kiss could last more than three seconds. This severely hampered the more morally ambiguous Westerns, and *Cimarron* would likely have fallen foul of the restrictions. It also means that some of the earliest talkies are grittier than ones made a decade later.

Which leads us to violence. Obviously, bloody wounds were not going to be tolerated, but there was even a formula for firing a gun. The cause and effect of violence must have a break in it to pass the code. Imagine a scene where the gunslinger (facing the camera) pulls out his gun and fires. Then there's a new image of a man doubling over, wincing in pain.

The two shots are separate, but the mind works out that the gun fired in image one has hit the target in image two. What you can't have is a gunslinger in the foreground, back to the camera, blasting away at a guy in the background who falls over dead. It's all one scene; the cause and effect of the gunshot are seamless. That level of violence broke the code and would be edited out or banned. Sergio Leone had no knowledge of this rule. He filmed his action the second way, which explains why *A Fistful of Dollars* got an instant reputation for being brutal. Today the film is not considered to be excessive in its depiction of violence.

In 1935 (during the Hays Code era), *Annie Oakley* hit the big screen. It starred Barbara Stanwyck and was directed by George Stevens. Stanwyck was a big star at the time but had never been in a Western, and the film elevated her from a slump caused by recent, lesser movies. The real Annie Oakley (born Phoebe Ann Mosey) had died in 1926, so the film wasn't about some long dead pioneer but someone people would have remembered.

The real Oakley came from a very poor family, so to supplement their income she was trapping small prey by the age of seven and hunting with a gun by the age of eight. She was never part of the Wild West, had nothing to do with law enforcement and never fired a gun at a Native American, but she was such a good shot (it was a novelty for a woman to be good with a rifle) that Buffalo Bill added her to his show and she became a sensation. Edison recorded her marksmanship on film in 1894, and she appeared in a few films. There are photos of her firing a rifle over her shoulder and hitting the mark by looking at a mirror. It was an impressive stunt, but she was more novelty act than anything to do with the Wild West. In 1901, she was involved in a train accident and had to undergo five spinal operations to stop potential paralysis. It is said that she taught more than 15,000 women how to shoot as she felt passionately that it kept the mind active and, more practically, it helped women know how to defend themselves. In 1898, she offered to lead fifty female sharpshooters into battle when the Spanish-American War broke out. President Mckinley didn't reply.

Perhaps her most famous feat occurred in Europe, not America. In 1890, in the Buffalo Bill Show, part of her routine involved asking for a volunteer from the crowd to put a cigarette in their mouth so she could shoot it from their lips (today, the number of health and safety issues around this would mean it could not be performed). This was all done for real, and in the event nobody volunteered, her husband (who was also a great sharpshooter) would step in. However, in Germany in 1890, Kaiser Wilhelm II, who had already seen the show and was a big fan of Oakley's volunteered. She did exactly what she promised and shot the cigarette from his lips. The stunt made both Wilhelm and Annie look good, and they got a tremendous round of applause. Twenty-four years later, at the outbreak of World War I, Oakley went on record to say she could have stopped the war had she missed the cigarette and shot the Kaiser instead. It's one of history's great "what ifs".

The film *Annie Oakley* therefore portrays the life of a woman who became famous in showbusiness and was one of the first women to appear regularly on film now being re-enacted in the same medium less than a decade after her death. The movie, of course, takes huge liberties with her life, but the general tone is reverential and, broadly speaking, doesn't exaggerate her deeds. Because the lead was a woman, the film fixates more on her romance with her eventual husband than all the sharpshooting she did. *Annie Oakley* got great reviews and was a big hit at the time; and it's pretty good by modern standards, with Stanwyck coming across as completely comfortable in the title role. What's interesting is this film is almost a metacommentary on the mythmaking of the Old West. While this was not the intended subtext of the movie, it clearly shows the artifice that was creeping into the retelling of these stories. Oakley was part of the Wild West Show; she wasn't part of the story of the Wild West.

Annie Oakley gave Stanwyck's career a whole new lease of life. She would go on not only to act in more Western movies such as *Cattle Queen of Montana* or *Forty Guns*, but to give a real renaissance to Westerns by appearing in the classic TV series *Rawhide*, *Wagon Train* and *The Big Valley (*where she appeared in 112 episodes). Her last role was that of Constance Colby in *Dynasty* and *The Colbys* when she was in her seventies.

One of the last events of the Old West was the Klondike Gold Rush. This was a mass movement of people to the Klondike region of the Yukon, not in America but Canada, between 1896 and 1899. Local miners discovered gold in the summer of 1896. When the news reached Seattle and San Francisco the following year, it led to a flood of 100,000 prospectors into the region. A few got lucky and became wealthy, but the majority came away with nothing. The Yukon isn't far from the Arctic Circle and its winters are brutal, so now we have a Western story that is all wrong (according to the stereotype): the wrong country, lots of snow and prospectors, rather than the American West, desert and cowboys.

Call of the Wild was also released in 1935. It was an adaptation of a 1903 novel of the same name by Jack London. Clark Gable played the lead, a man who is down on his luck but hears of the discovery of gold in the Yukon, so he pays $250 for Buck, a savage St Bernard dog, and a sled to help him through the snow. The film is about an animal and a man struggling against the elements. (The studios had known since the start that audiences liked to see animals onscreen. Warner Bros may have more than a century-long legacy of amazing movies, but that doesn't change the fact that their first bankable star in the 1920s was Rin Tin Tin, a dog. Tom Mix also proved the popularity of animals with his horse Tony.) The love interest was played by Loretta Young, who it turned out, fell pregnant from her fling with Gable. Fifty years later, Young confided to her family that the fling was the very "definition of date rape". She was only twenty-two, and Gable was already a big star, but those facts were not known in 1935.

The movie got great reviews and made a lot of money, further cementing Gable's huge popularity. A mere eighty-five years later it was remade in 2020, this time starring Harrison Ford and an inexplicably animated dog. I have discussed this trio of movies from the 1930s to completely pushback on the idea that all Westerns are the same and underline how the genre is amazingly flexible. None of the movies revolve around either lawmen or outlaws. *Cimarron* is the story of a smalltown newspaper editor, Oakley did a lot of shooting, but never in anger, and the point of *Call of the Wild* is man overcoming nature. The heroes of these movies are a journalist, an entertainer and a prospector, which sounds kind of westerny until you remember that the movie is set in Canada, and everyone is freezing in the sub-zero temperatures.

A lot of important Westerns have so far been discussed, but let's be honest by acknowledging that they are all rather obscure. So, let's get to our first bonafide classic, which is still watched today. Even if you haven't seen it, you will know something about it. In 1939, the same year *Gone with the Wind* was released, *Stagecoach* also came out. As mentioned in the section about Tom Mix, John Wayne had been working for years on the periphery of the Hollywood film industry, but this film was his big break. Already thirty-two, he played the Ringo Kid, and a legend was born when the camera zoomed in on him and he cocked his rifle. John Ford's early career has also been mentioned, but *Stagecoach* was the first of his classic Westerns, most of which starred John Wayne.

Wayne had gone from prop boy and general runner to bit-part player by 1926/7. His rise to stardom took years. Indeed, even his name went through various iterations. He was born in 1907, weighing a colossal thirteen pounds! He was named Marion Robert Morrison, but Wayne claims it was switched to Marion Michael Morrison after the birth of his brother who was named Robert, so even in his infancy there were name changes. While working in the props department for Fox Film Corporation, he got a leading man role in 1930's *The Big Trail* (his salary rose to $105 a week; compare that to Tom Mix's $20,000 in the same year), but a leading tough guy can't be called Marion. Director Raoul Walsh suggested "Anthony Wayne", but Fox Chief Executive Winfield Sheehan rejected it as sounding "too Italian". Then Walsh suggested "John Wayne" which Sheehan liked. The irony is that Marion Morrison was not even present for the discussion. So the name Wayne, which is forever associated with him, wasn't his or even chosen by him. But what about that enduring nickname "The Duke"? It seems Wayne had a bit part in 1929's *Words and Music* and was given his onscreen credit as "Duke Morrison", and the rest, as they say, is history. The final irony is that while John Ford and John Wayne are forever associated with classic Westerns, those weren't the real names of either of them.

Stagecoach is based on a 1937 book called The Stage to Lordsburg by Ernest Haycox. It was not a cultural phenomenon like *Gone with the Wind*, but its impact on moviemaking was enormous. The film is a tightly paced, white knuckle story about a group of strangers who have to survive a stagecoach journey through hostile territory. This is a widely used, basic premise that could result in *Wages of Fear*, or the average submarine movie, or the truck chase scene in *Raiders of the Lost Ark*. Wayne's character is an outlaw who is making the journey in handcuffs. Does the group use his skills and risk him turning the gun on them, or do they keep him locked up, meaning he remains a liability? The dilemma is a standard one, seen as recently as 2023's *Plane*. Today these are all movie tropes, but at the time, this was fresh, pressure-cooker storytelling. It's why this film still works today.

By 1939, Wayne still wasn't a big star; he'd had leading roles in a few lesser films but was still, at times, relegated to a supporting role. He just hadn't caught fire ... yet. That all changed with *Stagecoach*. Wayne was not the lead actor, just part of an ensemble cast, but the film crackles to life with his arrival, and now we see Wayne as the quintessential movie star (which is different to screen actor). When you pay to see a John Wayne movie, you want him playing his laconic good guy with his distinctive burr. Anything else and it would be a flop (like the time he played Genghis Khan in *The Conqueror*). He knew what audiences wanted and gave it to them, whether he was playing a cowboy, pilot, marine or firefighter. There is a throughline of this star power from Tom Mix to John Wayne and on to later movie stars like Arnold Schwarzenegger or Dwayne "The Rock" Johnson. It had taken twelve years, but Marion Morrison finally became John Wayne "The Legend" in this movie. That's not to say the relationship between Ford and

Wayne was one of friendly respect. Ford was notorious for bullying his actors to get the performances he wanted. Everyone took their share of abuse, including Wayne. Ford literally referred to him as a "big oaf" and a "dumb bastard". On one occasion Ford grabbed Wayne by the chin and shook him, asking, "Why are you moving your mouth so much? Don't you know you don't act with your mouth in pictures? You act with your eyes". We may debate the methods, but there's no debating the finished film. Ford was trying to make Wayne a strong, silent type and it worked. The impression that Wayne makes in the film is created by giving him plenty of expressive reaction shots throughout.

For the first time Ford decided to film in Monument Valley, famous for its giant butte formations which make the landscape appear almost alien. He fell in love with this location and used it again and again in his later movies. But this wasn't the only location he used in the film. Indeed, you don't need to be an expert in fauna and flora to tell that the scenery changes quite a lot for this particular stagecoach journey.

Forget artistic endeavour, technically, *Stagecoach* is a great film, starting with the claustrophobic atmosphere as the passengers are threatened by attack from all sides. The stunt work carried out by Yakima Canutt is breathtaking, particularly the truly terrifying scene where the Apache warrior falls between the galloping horses and lies dead on the ground as the stagecoach goes straight over his body (Steven Spielberg would honour this in the truck scene in *Raiders of the Lost Ark* forty years later). Canutt later explained in an interview how he did it: "You have to run the horses fast...When you turn loose to go under the coach, you've got to bring your arms over your chest and stomach. You've got to hold your elbows close to your body, or that front axle will knock them off." When Canutt asked Ford if he got the shot he wanted, Ford replied yes, but later said he would have lied if he'd had to because now that he had seen the stunt he was certain that Canutt would be killed on a second take. This is a rip-roaring adventure if ever there was one. Even though the back projection isn't very convincing to today's viewer, Orson Wells thought it was the epitome of filmmaking and watched it forty times to prepare for his directorial debut *Citizen Kane*.

Stagecoach, like many of the movies at the time, has the spectre of racism hanging over it. Even though the film is not a polemic about Native Americans, its depiction of them as unmotivated bad guys offends today's audiences. In Westerns, it's the good guys versus the bad guys and the only goal is to entertain. The problem is that the bad guys portrayed are a real people (most often played by white actors, which adds another layer of racism). *Stagecoach* was not deliberately trying to offend, rather the attitudes portrayed are a reflection of society at the time.

The film came out to rave reviews and cleaned up at the box office. It was nominated for a slew of Oscars and won two: Best Music/Score and Best Supporting Actor for Thomas Mitchell as Doc Josiah Boone. The wins are especially impressive considering this was the year of *Mr Smith Goes to Washington*, *Gone with the Wind*, *Wuthering Heights*, *Goodbye, Mr. Chips* and *The Wizard of Oz*. The place of *Stagecoach* in cinema history was cemented in every possible way.

World War II didn't stop Hollywood although the ramping up of patriotic war movies became the obvious direction to go. The moviegoer of the day was more likely to be entertained by shooting Nazis than shooting Native Americans. That said, next up on the Western scene is Howard Hawks' *Red River*, starring John Wayne. The movie was filmed in 1946, trademarked in 1947, but not released until 1948. This is strange because despite Hawks and John Wayne being reliable names in terms of generating box office cash, the studio sat on the film for two years. *Red River* is loosely based on some real history which is merely the inspiration for the actual story the filmmakers want to tell. Superficially, it's about the first cattle drive from Texas to Kansas along the Chisholm Trail. In reality, it's a remake of mutiny on the Bounty only with cows and with Wayne playing a cowpoke version of Captain Bligh. This black and white film (Hawks regarded Technicolor as "too garish") was both a critical and commercial success but ran into controversy over the ending, which was said to be too similar to 1943's *The Outlaw*. This has led to multiple versions of it appearing on TV and home release.

When John Ford saw *Red River* he was impressed with Wayne's performance, saying, "I never knew the big son-of-a-bitch could act". This led to Ford casting Wayne in more complex, multi-layered and dramatic roles, reaching a pinnacle with *The Searchers*, a film that will come up in the next chapter. However in 1946, almost immediately after the war, Ford made another classic, *My Darling Clementine*. The film starred Henry Fonda, who played Wyatt Earp, and recreated the famous shoot-out at the OK Corral. What's interesting is that the film's promotional material highlights Ford's Oscar win but also mentions *Stagecoach*, despite the movie being seven years old and not a movie Ford won an Oscar for, which shows the impact of that film on moviegoing audiences of the time. Once again Monument Valley is the location, and once again there are tense gunfights, but the canvas this time is much broader. Wyatt Earp lived into the 1920s and met some of the early Western stars. He was in the rare situation of being able to act as an advisor to the producers of some of the earliest movies about that famous gunfight. It's impossible to know what a person is thinking, but anyone human must be tempted to tell the best version of the events, particularly the ones that made them famous.

Reports from the Gunfight at the OK Corral are quite telling in that these men, who knew their way around a pistol, had to be extremely close to each other to stand any chance of hitting anything. It's the same reason why soldiers formed long lines to fire away at the enemy in the US Civil War or in the Napoleonic era, and it's all to do with physics. Firing a gun is a form of controlled explosion. A charge goes off behind a projectile, and that bullet then hurtles down the barrel of the gun. If the gun barrel is just a metal tube, that projectile will ricochet off the inside of the barrel, and while the shot will fire out of the gun, exactly which direction it will go is anybody's guess. This is why those long lines of musket men were so important. The bullets would be sent flying in so many different trajectories you needed fifty guys firing at the same time to hit any of the enemy soldiers right in front of you. The Brown Bess (the standard British infantry musket from the 1720s through to about 1850) was effective at a maximum range of just 100 yards, and other armies' rifles were no better.

Revolvers like the Colt Navy pistol or the later Colt Single Action Army pistol were the classic Wild West guns. Both had those smooth barrels, which meant they faced the same problem, only more so, as pistols generally aren't as accurate as muskets. The problem was remedied with the invention of rifling, an arrangement of spiral grooves on the inside of the barrel. Now, as the bullet travels down the barrel, it spins, which means it doesn't bounce along the barrel and is therefore far more accurate. Now it was possible to hit the intended target. As for the classic shooting of the noose at a hanging …how many times has this been reported by eyewitnesses in all the reliable tales of the Wild West? The answer is never and it's for very good reasons: First, hitting a rope from 300 yards would be an almost impossible shot with any gun. Second, a bullet (of any reasonable calibre) isn't as wide as a piece of rope, which means it simply cannot cut the rope cleanly. I saw a documentary in which a special forces sniper tried to do it, but he only managed to hit the rope once. His hit took out a chunk of the rope, but the hanging dummy was not released from its grim fate. He said that the only way to do it is to perfectly cut one side out with one bullet and then do the same, to millimetre perfection, on the other side, something he believed was simply impossible. But he didn't allow for Hollywood ingenuity which perfected the trick by tying the noose around a small explosive charge and running a wire up the rope. When the charge is triggered, it severs the rope cleanly every time.

The exact events of the gunfight are debated to this day as there are multiple conflicting reports. Saying that, a number of eyewitnesses are in agreement about what happened overall and give a good account of how that deadly thirty seconds unfolded. The Earp brothers (Virgil, Wyatt and Morgan) were not expecting a fight. Trouble with the local gangs of outlaw cowboys led by Frank McLaury and Billy Clanton had been simmering for a while, but during a court case that morning the men had apparently been disarmed. However, Doc Holliday had a short coach gun concealed under his long jacket just in case, and Billy Clanton and Frank McLaury had revolvers in their holsters as they stood alongside their saddled horses with rifles in their packs. When Virgil saw the cowboys, he testified that he immediately ordered them to "Throw up your hands, I want your guns!" Virgil and Wyatt both testified they saw Frank McLaury and Billy Clanton draw and cock their single-action, six-shot revolvers. Virgil yelled, "Hold! I don't mean that!

Who started shooting first is not certain; accounts by both participants and eyewitnesses are contradictory. Smoke from black gunpowder used in the weapons added to the confusion in the narrow street, but the six or seven men with guns fired about thirty shots in around thirty seconds. Virgil Earp reported afterward, "Two shots went off right together. Billy Clanton's was one of them." Wyatt testified, "Billy Clanton levelled his pistol at me, but I did not aim at him. I knew that Frank McLaury had the reputation of being a good shot and a dangerous man, and I aimed at Frank McLaury." He said he shot Frank McLaury after both he and Billy Clanton went for their revolvers: "The first two shots were fired by Billy Clanton and myself, he shooting at me, and I shooting at Frank McLaury." Clanton missed, but Earp shot Frank McLaury in the stomach.

General firing immediately broke out. Virgil and Wyatt thought Tom McLaury (Frank's brother) was armed. When the shooting started, the horse that Tom held jumped to one side, and Wyatt said he saw Tom throw his hand to his right hip. Holliday drew the coach gun from under his long coat, stepped around Tom McLaury's horse and shot him in the chest at close range with a double-barrelled shotgun. The unarmed Tom stumbled away from the gunfight and fell down dead at the foot of a telegraph pole. Holliday tossed the empty shotgun aside, pulled out his nickel-plated revolver and continued to fire at Frank McLaury and Billy Clanton.

Ike Clanton (Billy's brother) had been publicly threatening to kill the Earps for several months, including issuing very loud threats the day before. However, when the gunfight broke out, Clanton ran forward and grabbed Wyatt, exclaiming that he was unarmed and did not want a fight. To this protest Wyatt said he responded, "Go to fighting or get away!" Ike Clanton ran through the front door of Fly's boarding house and escaped unharmed. Though wounded, Billy Clanton and Frank McLaury kept shooting. One of them, perhaps Billy, fired a shot at Morgan Earp that caught him across the back and created a wound that injured both shoulder blades and a vertebra. Morgan went down for a minute before picking himself up. Either Frank or Billy shot Virgil Earp in the calf. Virgil, though hit, fired his next shot at Billy Clanton.

Frank, now across the street and still walking at a good pace despite his wound, fired twice more before he was shot in the head under his right ear. Billy Clanton was shot in the wrist, chest and abdomen, and after a minute or two, slumped to a sitting position near his original place, where he continued to fire with the pistol supported on his leg. After he ran out of ammunition, he called for more cartridges, but he had his pistol taken away, which ended the shooting.

This is an amazingly detailed description of perhaps the most famous shootout in history, but even if the events were filmed in slow motion that's a minute and half of a movie that you have to build another ninety minutes (at least) around. *My Darling Clementine* decides to take this carefully researched information and throw it all away, even getting the year of the shootout wrong. While getting the date wrong is inexcusable, the main reason for the errors is the books Ford used to research the history around the famous shootout. They weren't exactly highbrow academic tomes even by the standards of the day and are now dismissed as lacking any credibility. It is worth noting that Wyatt Earp contributed to them, and so we have the first piece of hard evidence that he was instrumental in creating his own legend.

The primary issue with all so-called historical films is that they are not obliged to stick to the facts. They are entertainment first and historical accuracy is of secondary importance. *My Darling Clementine* is certainly entertaining, and some viewers may not even realise that it's based on real events, so it's mission accomplished by all involved. In this instance the female lead, who is supposedly the girlfriend of Doc Holliday, is entirely made up. Her name is Chihuahua, and she is meant to be Mexican but is played by Linda Darnell, so the whole role is culturally insensitive. Victor Mature plays Doc Holliday and appears to be in rude good health for someone who was dying of tuberculosis, but that was alright because in this version he dies in the gunfight. It's almost as if a decision was made to get everything wrong, and yet it is widely considered to be one of the greatest Westerns ever made. It's not a factual account of what took place but a legendary version of that era in American history. A quote from the last film in this chapter, *The Man Who Shot Liberty Valance*, could be a summary of this entire book: "When the legend becomes fact, print the legend". *My Darling Clementine* got rave reviews, was a big box office hit and has largely aged very well - if you ignore the total lack of historical accuracy and the whitewashing of one character.

In 1948, John Ford reunited with John Wayne to make *Fort Apache*, the first of the "cavalry trilogy", each separated by a year. The others are 1949's *She Wore a Yellow Ribbon* and 1950's *Rio Grande*. In all these films Ford directs, and Wayne plays different roles in the US cavalry. The phrase "here comes the cavalry" comes from these films as each portrays images of brave cavalry soldiers charging into battle, bugles blaring, to save the day. Of the three, *Fort Apache* is generally considered to be the best. Wayne and Ford had already shot plenty of native warriors in *Stagecoach*, but it's these films that underline the indifference mid-20th century white Americans had to the complexities of the settler relationship with the indigenous peoples. Taken for what they are, they are brilliant pieces of entertainment, but once again, we have First Nation peoples portrayed as the faceless enemy and are given a paternalistic and patronising view of their culture. To use today's terminology, they are othered.

Fort Apache featured John Wayne, Henry Fonda and Shirley Temple, three massive stars, all in one movie. Temple was no longer a little girl but at twenty was a fresh-faced young woman married to John Agar who made his screen debut in this film. Ford bullied him mercilessly, even calling him "Mr Temple" in front of the cast and crew. Wayne took him under his wing and helped Agar weather the storm. It's interesting to note that the promotional material for the film used photos of a much younger Shirley Temple to remind the audience of her childhood heyday.

The film is based on the 1947 short story by James Warner Bellah with the much blunter name, Massacre. The short story isn't about any specific historical event but is clearly influenced by two notable defeats of the US Army by Native Americans: the Fetterman Fight of 1866 and the Battle of Little Bighorn in 1876. On both occasions US forces were all but wiped out, and on both occasions it was down to the hubris of the US Army officers in charge.

Fort Apache is set in the titular fort, deep in native territory, shortly after the American Civil War. Captain Kirby York (Wayne) is expected to replace the outgoing commander and his years of experience dealing with the local tribes; his firm but fair treatment of the men means he's the right man for the job. However, overall command of the garrison is given to Lieutenant Colonel Owen Thursday (Fonda). A general during the civil war, he is known for his rash acts of bravery that have paid off in the past, but his arrogance has led to his demotion and a role he feels is beneath him. He is completely unsuited to dealing with the local tribes with their unique cultures and traditions. Perhaps he could instigate a crisis but save the day in a blaze of glory?

While the white Americans are yet again the good guys and the bad guys are the native people, the setup is more nuanced than that and quite clever. Both Ford and Wayne have been criticised for their politics (as we shall see in the next film), but that's not to say they treated their nation's history as beyond criticism. There are a few films where Wayne plays a character who is the calming presence, the voice of reason in the face of unreasonableness, and this film is the perfect example. Almost everything Thursday does is wrong, but he is the superior officer. York tries to guide him, but Thursday's hubris doesn't allow him to see it. The film shows that when the wrong man is promoted to a position of power, dire consequences can result. In this regard it's a morally complex story.

The film culminates with Thursday provoking the Apaches into battle. He leaves York behind, which leads to the massacre of Thursday's forces, and York is surrounded but released by the Apaches because he is an honourable man. The last scene takes place a few years later when York is now in charge of the fort. He is discussing the famous painting of "Thursday's Charge" with a journalist, and while York condemns Thursday, he says that as long as the regiment lives, the men who lost their lives will never be forgotten. It's an interesting ending which would have provided food for thought to the post-war audience. It was certainly brave of Ford to portray US military incompetence only a few years after millions of men had been demobilised at the end of World War II. At the same time some of those men would have recognised an inferior officer putting men in harm's way. All of that said, the film takes time to pay its respects to the men of the armed services, and in the safe hands of John Wayne, we know everything is going to be alright. *Fort Apache* was a big hit at the box office and often gets into the top ten or twenty Westerns of all time.

However, going back to the concept of what constitutes a Western, *Fort Apache* fits none of the usual stereotypes. There are no cowboys in this movie. John Wayne and everyone else are in the US army fighting the Apache nation. Critics consider this to be a Western, but as there are two groups of warriors clashing on the field of battle, would the genre 'war film' be more appropriate? It's yet another reminder of how arbitrary genre definitions can be.

As magnificent as *My Darling Clementine* or *Fort Apache* are, there was a later film that eclipsed them in every possible way, 1952's *High Noon*. We are now into the 1950s when colour movies had been a regular feature in cinemas for more than a dozen years. So why is this film in black and white? The answer is the director Fred Zinnemann. He started shooting in colour but didn't like it, saying it wasn't sombre enough for the story he wanted to tell. In the 50s, while colour was on the rise, not all films were shot that way, so he had the artistic flexibility to change the entire cinematography of the movie, and it worked.

The background to this film was the deeply disturbing events taking place in the House of Representatives' Un-American Activities Committee (HUAC). It was created to investigate alleged disloyalty and subversive activities on the part of private citizens, public employees and those organizations suspected of having communist ties, which led to the infamous question, "Are you, or have you ever been a member of the Communist Party?" This was at the start of the Cold War, when the Soviet Union, led by Joseph Stalin, had just created its first nuclear bomb. Anyone appearing before the committee had good reason to be worried because just being interviewed pretty much guaranteed an end to their career. It was guilt by association and as the Communist Party was not illegal, it was also the intimidation of political beliefs. It is one of the darkest chapters in American politics. In Hollywood it led to a 20th century witch-hunt as the more liberal and left-leaning movie industry had disproportionally more communists and communist sympathisers than the general population, resulting in an equally disproportionate impact on the way other Americans viewed Hollywood. The movie industry was under the microscope in ways it had never been before.

One of the casualties of this era was the screenwriter Carl Foreman who had once been a member of the Communist Party, but when interviewed by HUAC, he declined to identify fellow members or anyone he suspected of current membership. As a result, he was labelled an "uncooperative witness", and blacklisted, meaning he could no longer work in the industry. Foreman and Stanley Kramer had made several films together, but now Kramer demanded an immediate dissolution of the partnership. This is highlighted in a later documentary which lays all the blame for the failure of the partnership at Kramer's feet, but a kinder reading would be, quite simply, that he was a businessman and his partner had just become toxic. To give some kind of modern context, it was like the #MeToo movement: once accused, your past reputation was irrelevant as no one was going to work with you moving forwards. As a signatory to the production loan, Foreman remained with the *High Noon* project, but before the film's release, he sold his partnership share to Kramer and moved to Britain. His career in America was over.

In *High Noon*, the town marshal is looking for help from the local people only to find all of them politely abandoning him and leaving him to fend for himself, an obvious metaphor for the fate of Foreman and others. John Wayne had originally been offered the lead role but refused it because he believed that Foreman's story was an obvious allegory against blacklisting, which as a Republican, he actively supported. Gary Cooper was chosen instead. Cooper was fifty-one and past his prime in terms of star power, but the film was so successful it reenergised his career. In the film Cooper plays Marshal Will Kane, the lawman in Hadleyville, New Mexico. He knows that when the train arrives at noon there will be killers onboard, and they will be coming to get him. The movie is revolutionary in many ways, not least because it is filmed almost in real time, and as bad as the gunman are, they are not as unstoppable or as inevitable as the march of time, the real enemy.

And then there's Grace Kelly's role. Up to this point women in Westerns were usually the damsel in distress or the hooker with a heart of gold, but Grace's role has more agency and gives us a woman to admire in a genre usually about six-shooters and men sleeping with their horses. In this film she is married to Cooper, and as a Quaker and therefore a pacifist, her solution is simple: leave town, avoid trouble. In the end, she renounces her pacifism to help her husband. The concept of the mail-order bride evolved in the frontier era. Women who wanted to escape the crushingly claustrophobic patriarchy in the East headed West, hoping to find more freedom to better control their lives. So, this strong female character is likely to have been more reflective of the norm than Westerns set in the 40s and 50s would have us think. The film also marks the screen debut of an actor who would become synonymous with tough guy/bad man roles in Westerns, Lee Van Cleef. Although he has no lines of dialogue he conveys his character by looking suitably menacing throughout.

Finally, *High Noon* is an early example of a revisionist Western, quietly revolutionary in its own way. The narrative in many Westerns is that of the settlers bringing "civilisation" to the Wild West. I don't have a chapter to debate this, so let's just say it was a lot more complicated than that. However, just when the marshal needs them most, the townspeople melt away, and Marshal Will Kane is left very much on his own. It's tense viewing even today.

The initial response to the film was one of confusion. John Wayne called the movie "the most un-American thing I've ever seen in my whole life" and went on to make *Rio Bravo* (coming up in the next chapter) as a direct response to *High Noon*. So, we have a movie set in a historical period which does nothing to accurately reflect that period but is a perfect encapsulation of the time in which it was made. It eschews the sweeping vistas of a Ford film and is, instead, a claustrophobic character study, light on action (until the end). It feels more like a thriller than a Western, and yet once people began to understand what was there, rather than what wasn't, they loved it. The new Republican President Eisenhower loved it. The Democratic President Bill Clinton loved it and screened it more than a dozen times in the White House more than forty years later. It was a box office hit and was nominated for seven Oscars, winning four, including Best Actor for Gary Cooper.

The last of the great black and white Westerns was 1962's *The Man Who Shot Liberty Valance*, directed by John Ford. By the 1960s almost everything was in colour. I have to confess that when I first saw the film, I presumed it was shot in the late 40s, as why have a Western in black and white in the year *Lawrence of Arabia* came out? The answer is a virtual cottage industry. Ford said in an interview, "In black and white, you've got to be very careful. You've got to know your job, lay your shadows in properly, get your perspective right, but in colour, there it is ... You might say I'm old fashioned, but black and white is real photography". But then there is the notion that like *High Noon*, this is a revisionist Western and that a return to black and white makes the film feel older and grittier. These almost poetic reasons are a little suspicious as Hollywood is notoriously about the bottom line rather than poetry. According to cinematographer William H Clothier, "There was one reason and one reason only …Paramount was cutting costs". So, whether you want to believe that this was Ford's fond farewell to the genre that had defined him (although he would sneak in a couple more before his death) or the bean counters restricting the budget, the answer is up to you.

The story in *The Man Who Shot Liberty Valance* revolves around a lawyer and a rancher. When US Senator Ransom Stoddard attends the funeral of local rancher Tom Doniphon, questions are raised about the titular main event, which is recounted in flashback by the senator, a lawyer years ago when Doniphon saved him from the notorious local outlaw Liberty Valance. When Stoddard arrives in town, Doniphon befriends him and teaches him how to shoot. Even the local marshal is afraid of Valance, so the town essentially belonged to the outlaw to do with as he will. Over time Stoddard builds up the courage to confront Valance, but when he is easily overcome, it is Doniphon who kills Valance and saves his friend. The men allow everyone to think that Stoddard killed Valance, which leads to his rise to fame and his career as a senator, but as the journalist in the film understands, this lie, if revealed, would jeopardise Stoddard's reputation and career. This is the origin of the previously quoted line, "When the legend becomes fact, print the legend".

Stoddard is played by James Stewart, Doniphon is played by John Wayne, and Liberty Valance is played by Lee Marvin (Lee Van Cleef gets a bigger role this time around). While Ford and Wayne had been working together for more than twenty years, this shoot was hard. Paramount had demanded that Wayne be used as Doniphon (to be fair to the studio, Wayne was perfect for the role and he's great in the movie), but because the choice was forced on him, Ford turned the full force of his bullying abuse on Wayne. Perhaps his nastiest comments were his accusations about Wayne not enlisting in World War II. Ford had been wounded in the Battle of Midway, and Stewart had flown bomber sorties over Europe. "How rich did you get while Jimmy was risking his life?" he taunted at one point. Woody Strode, one of the few perennial Black actors in Westerns at the time, generally avoided abuse but described it as a miserable experience because it felt like everyone was in a bad mood. According to Strode everyone was bickering with everyone else, but it was Ford who started it and created the toxic work environment.

The film came out to great reviews and made a load of money, so mission accomplished, but for most of those involved it was an experience best forgotten. The story of *The Man Who Shot Liberty Valance* is not based on any real history, so in a way, this is the perfect place to end the chapter. The picture is about memory, about how facts are twisted to become legends, and legends settle in to become truths. Sergio Leone, a huge fan of Ford and this film, observed that this was the one time Ford had a pessimistic world view. The journalist in the movie knows the truth but also understands that hard facts aren't always what people want. It's the same for the movies: a cowboy's life was repetitive and uneventful; the days were long and dull. Cowboys were more likely to wear a derby (a bowler hat in Britain) than a ten-gallon hat, but that wasn't what the public paid to see. People want to relive the legends, they want to see the myths, and Hollywood obliges time and time again.

Chapter 3

Filmed in Technicolor

The simply named movie *The Viking* came out in 1928. It is neither a Western nor a cinema classic, but it is important. It was the first-ever movie filmed in colour and with sound, although it only had a musical score: there was no dialogue. But from this humble and experimental beginning evolved the industry standard as today almost all motion pictures are in colour, with sound. In fact, if either is missing, it's unusual enough to be of note. The first colour Western with sound was released in the 1930s. *Whoopee!* is a musical based on the 1928 stage show, and it was shot in two colours. This makes it one of the oldest colour films with sound ever made and one of the first movie musicals. It was a Western, a musical, a comedy, and it had dancing choreographed by a young Busby Berkeley. This film launched his stellar career.

Whoopee! was a slightly raunchy pre-code film. The song My Baby Just Cares for Me, immortalised more than a generation later by Nina Simone, is from this musical. It was the number one box office hit of the year in America, and yet, this film has been completely forgotten. So, while Westerns weren't the first in either colour or sound or the first to bring them together, they were one of the pioneers of the genre. Strangely though, we have jumped back more than thirty years from the last entry of the black and white Westerns, but having colour brought a whole new layer of realism to the movies.

The problem with colour movies in the 30s and 40s (as I point out in my book Hollywood and History: What the Movies Get Wrong from Ancient Greece to Vietnam) is that in this era, colour wasn't subtle. The blues are BLUE and the reds are RED, so while it's an improvement on the monochromatic past, colour hadn't yet developed to a realistic portrayal of what our eyes see every day. However, this is a period that most people think of as one of Classic Westerns. As this book has shown, if that were the case, there would be a lot of great films that got pushed to one side, but there's no doubt that it was instead a time of mass marketing, when the studios were churning out genre movies of wildly varying quality, budgets and messages.

Moving forward a few years to 1939, we have *Dodge City*, starring Errol Flynn, a movie proudly filmed in Technicolor. Flynn was the quintessential matinee idol: good looking, physically fit enough to do his own stunts and always playing the most dashing of heroes. He could make any woman swoon. Flynn was like John Wayne (Wayne was only two years his senior) in that both men tended to play the same role again and again. Flynn was born in Australia but didn't have the accent as he had attended school in England where he started his film career. His accent, whether intended or not, was decidedly clipped, upper-class English. He also maintained the same pencil moustache, regardless of the era. This worked well when he was playing Captain Blood or a cavalry officer in *Charge of the Light Brigade* and even more so as Robin Hood, but as a veteran of the US Civil War or a gunslinging cowboy? Not so much. But like Wayne, people expected the star to be the same star, just in a different costume, fighting a different injustice. The stories were nothing new, whether about the railroad coming to town or the law dealing with gangs of outlaws. The films were a veritable list of cliches, but that didn't matter; if the stars appeared as expected, the effort was rewarded at the box office.

To be fair to Flynn, *Dodge City* was his first Western, and he was worried whether people would buy him as a cowboy. Olivia de Havilland, who had starred with Flynn in *Captain Blood* and *The Adventures of Robin Hood*, was once again paired with Flynn to recreate a successful partnership, and his fears were proved wrong. After a clever PR stunt to launch the film in the real Dodge City, with the cast arriving on a steam train to great fanfare and huge crowds, it turned out to be Warner Bros' biggest hit of the year. On the one hand, the film shows a complete lack of originality; on the other hand, the studio was smart enough to give the audience what it wanted, and it worked. For Olivia de Havilland, 1939 would be her best-ever year after having a major role in both *Dodge City* and *Gone with the Wind*. De Havilland lived to the ripe old age of 104 and died in 2020.

Interestingly, the very best Westerns from the 1940s were black and white. It was a transitional decade when the world was focused on World War II. The highlights of those films are explored in the previous chapter, but a standout omission is 1946's *Duel in the Sun*, directed by the as yet unmentioned King Vidor, who had an astonishing career starting in 1913 and continuing until 1980 (although his major motion picture career had ended by the late 1950s). The film is based on a popular 1944 novel of the same name. It's an unusual film in many respects, but its focus on a biracial woman (played by the very Caucasian Jennifer Jones) was something rarely seen at the time. In the story Pearl Chavez goes to live with white relations after her father murders her mother and is executed for his crime. Once with the new family in Texas she is tempted by the two sons, one good, the other bad, resulting in a steamy love triangle, the *Basic Instinct* of the day. Its portrayal of religion and sex led to numerous cuts as the Hays Code was broken regularly, although by today's standards it would be classified as a 12 in the UK or a PG-13 in America. A scene where Pearl does a seductive dance was considered so problematic they cut it entirely. After she is date raped, Pearl begins an abusive relationship with the bad brother. Her sexuality is seen as something that must be tamed. *Duel in the Sun* raises all kinds of issues familiar to today's audiences, but at a time when women were usually portrayed as asexual pillars of virtue, the exploration of female sexuality was both novel and shocking and reflected not only the changes taking place in society, but the changing role of women in wartime. Even after all the cuts, some American states still refused to show it. None of the previous movies discussed have had this level of contemporary controversy.

As a psychological Western, the story was complex, but the filming shouldn't have been. A train derailment was a major set piece, and hordes of galloping cowboys were needed in other scenes, but these things had been reproduced for decades. The screenwriter and producer was David O Selznick, only a few years away from his monster hit *Gone With the Wind*, and he poured as much grandiose effort into this film as that one. But filming was so out of control that it took a year and half, during which both VE and VJ Days took place (bringing World War II to a close). The issue seems to have been that because *Gone with the Wind* had been a licence to print money, nobody reigned in Selznick, and as the producer, he was in charge of the purse strings. The film finally came in around four times more than the cost of the average Western at the time. On top of that, Selznick launched a promotional campaign that added millions to the costs (more than enough to make an entire new movie). He bet big and he won big. *Duel in the Sun* was a box office smash. Cheekily, he even used the overruns as a sign of quality in the promotional material. The problem was the film had been so ruinously expensive (the cost was nearly double that of *Gone with the Wind*) that by the time the box office receipts had all come in, the film only just managed to squeak a profit. One of the advantages of the Western genre was being able to make a movie on a reasonable budget, but this one overran in every important respect. Quite simply, *Duel in the Sun* was not a movie that warranted being one of the most expensive films ever made (at the time).

A good example to prove the opposite in expenditure is 1950's *Colt .45*. This is a largely forgotten film starring Randolph Scott, an actor who was never going to worry the likes of John Wayne or Errol Flynn, but one who carved a niche for himself playing a reliable leading man in Westerns. Although his career lasted decades, he never made a stone-cold classic, and *Colt .45* is an example of his middling output. The story is simple enough: a gun seller is robbed of his stock (he should have utilised his wares) and vows to get his guns back. Indeed, the story of a stolen firearm leading to an adventure to get it back is suspiciously similar to the earlier released (and better regarded) Jimmy Stewart movie *Winchester '73*, only in this case it was a rifle rather than a brace of pistols. No great social statements, no genre-defining narrative. The whole film is run and done in 75 minutes, but it was not aspiring to be *Citizen Kane* or *Gone with the Wind*. It was cheap to make, it reused sets and costumes from other films … and it made a very healthy profit. There is no "art" here, only a product to be sold, and it sold well enough to make everyone involved some money. By 1950, Hollywood had been churning out cheap Westerns by the dozens for decades. Most have been rightly forgotten, so in a way, *Colt .45* is emblematic of the genre at the time.

The name *Colt .45* was deliberate because if there is one pistol any moviegoer will associate with a Western it's the Colt Single Action Army, also known as the Colt Peacemaker. Even during the era, there were many gunmakers, but Colt was seen as the Rolls Royce or the Cadillac of that era of firearms. Putting it bluntly, it's THAT revolver you will instantly recognise. The trouble is that it didn't come into service until 1873, which means that most of the frontier era wouldn't have had it. One of the first revolvers was the Colt Walker, designed in 1846, but because its co-creator died in battle in 1847, it wasn't extensively used (working originals are worth close to a million dollars – if you can find one). A far more common revolver was the Colt 1851 Navy Revolver, used extensively in the US Civil War by both sides, with more than 270,000 produced. So, for a cowboy in the 1860s, the Colt 1851 Navy Revolver would have been the standard firearm, and yet, they are much less commonly seen in Westerns (it's one of the rare moments of historical accuracy in the Dollars Trilogy but rather than loading them with black powder and ball shot, they use much later catridges).

In the movies, guns are worn in holsters low on the hip, ready for the quick draw. There are even some contemporary photos of cowboys and ranch hands wearing their pistols that way, but the pictures are posed; they were designed to enforce the myth that everyone wanted to see and believe (and were invariably done to impress a girl). By contrast, rare photos of these men at work on the plains show the guns in their belts, alongside the other tools of the job. Shootouts were surprisingly rare. A cowboy was more likely to use his gun to put down a lame cow or scare off some coyotes than to face a duel on the main street at high noon.

Next, we come to the 1951 movie *Distant Drums*. The film is set in Florida during the Second Seminole War and shows how far Gary Cooper had fallen before a year later starring in *High Noon*. *Distant Drums* was a typical cheap United States Pictures' movie churned out by the dozens that gave Westerns a bad name in the film critic community. Setting aside the casual racism and the fact that nobody bothered to find out anything about the firearms and uniforms of the 1830s/40s, it was obvious that all of the scenes were filmed in California on the studio lot or a sound stage.

Distant Drums tells the story of a daring military raid on a Spanish fort, followed by a chase through the dangerous Everglades by fearsome Seminole warriors and is the basis for a fun, sweaty historical thriller/Western/war film, but it was all done with minimum effort. It didn't get any critical attention when it came out, and it washed its face financially. So why mention such a mediocre movie? It's because of one sound effect. As Cooper leads his men through the swamp, an alligator moves in and takes down one of the men who lets out a primal screen. Studios are nothing if not budget conscious, and so, if they can sell off assets, in this case the primal scream, it's another way to ease budgets and make some money.

That scream was next used in 1953's *The Charge at Feather River*. This Western was an example of the 3D craze that swept American cinema for a few years in the 1950s. It meant that the actors were forever throwing things or loosing arrows out at the audience in an attempt to make full use of the (limited) technology in this otherwise forgotten film. The man killed by the alligator in *Distant Drums* was an unnamed extra, but this time his scream was put into the mouth of a Private Wilhelm as he is killed. Fast forwarding twenty-five years, a sound engineer called Ben Burtt liked the cry of anguish so much that he laid it over the death of a storm trooper in 1977's *Star Wars: Episode IV – A New Hope*. Burtt dubbed this sound bite "the Wilhelm scream" (although way too much effort has been put into finding the original recording, it appears to have come from a man called Sheb Wooley). And so, a cult cinematic in-joke was born. This same scream, originating as it did from a bad Gary Cooper Western, has been heard in such financially successful and critically acclaimed films as *The Lord of the Rings: The Two Towers*, *Toy Story*, *Reservoir Dogs*, *Captain America: Civil War*, *Raiders of the Lost Ark* and so on. This little aside is an example of an amusing influence Westerns had on Hollywood.

Early Westerns are not known for their diversity and inclusion, but how about a musical Western from the early 50s featuring lesbians? 1953's *Calamity Jane* stars the utterly clean-cut and delightful Doris Day playing Martha Jane Cannary, better known as Calamity Jane. This is such a tour de force of musical brio that you may not be aware she was a real person. Jane's life started as a reflection of the age. The family wanted to head west and establish themselves in the new lands recently opened up to settlers. It was a chance to make a better life for hundreds of thousands of people. However, by the age of fourteen, both parents were dead, so it was Jane's job to look after the rest of the family. She did this by taking every job she could get from dishwasher, to ox team driver, to occasional sex worker. By the age of twenty, Jane had become a scout for the US Army as it continued to clash with Native American tribes, and it was around this time she became known as Calamity Jane (there are multiple origin stories). For practical reasons, as she was riding, scouting and sometimes fighting, she wore men's clothing. A trouser-wearing, gun-toting female scout got the attention of the press and she became a celebrity. She was a part of the story of the Wild West and became one of the acts in Buffalo Bill's Wild West Show.

Jane ended up in Deadwood where she may have had a sexual relationship with Wild Bill Hickok. Even though she was an alcoholic, she was still involved in shootouts and was, at times, employed both as security and sex worker in the local brothel. She died aged fifty-one in

1903 from a combination of inflammation of the bowels (a symptom of her drinking) and pneumonia. Jane's is the sad story of a woman trying to earn a living and survive, but she caught the public imagination and still turns up in movies and TV shows.

None of this bleak narrative makes it into the 1953 movie. Instead, we get a glossy musical very loosely based on the supposed love affair between Jane and Hickock. However, at one point in the film Jane sets up home with another woman, and the joke is that she's the one literally wearing the trousers as they create a pseudo husband and wife relationship. It was never meant to be interpreted as a lesbian relationship, but this part of the film is pushed further into the realms of a sapphic metaphor as Jane sings "A Woman's Touch". To the modern viewer these women are clearly a couple, but at the time of filming, the setup was seen as an innocent joke.

Unlike a lot of onscreen musicals, *Calamity Jane* was not based on an existing stage musical. Instead, it was Warner Bros picking up on the success of the 1950 film *Annie Get Your Gun*, about the previously mentioned Annie Oakley. Doris Day was perfect for the role of Calamity Jane. She lowered her natural singing voice to sound tougher, and the standout song "Secret Love", for which she won an Oscar, she nailed in one take.

The film did solid business, won an Oscar and catapulted Day's star further into the stratosphere. Day later claimed it was the best on-set experience she ever had. More than most films from the 1950s, this one lives on and is regularly screened at LGBTQ movie festivals in the 21st century.

After some decidedly lesser films and a musical entry to the pantheon of Westerns, we come to 1953's *Shane*, a movie widely considered to be a classic of the genre and the most exciting movie ever made about agricultural land legislation. The plot centres around a gunslinger who wants to renounce his violent ways and arrives in town looking for a fresh start … but mostly it centres around the Homestead Acts. There were two primary ones: the first was passed in 1862 (nice to see the

US government had enough time during the Civil War to pass land reform legislation), and the second and potentially more important one was passed in 1866 after the war. This second act applied specifically to freed slaves so that African Americans could be part of this release of land in an area that was huge, about 160 million acres or roughly 10% of what today is the continental United States.

The Homestead Acts were an expression of northern politicians' desire to give individuals the opportunity to own their own land (160 acres), provided they undertook to improve it by farming, or homesteading as it was known. Successful applicants (in truth, anyone who applied) could acquire ownership of what had been federal land as a means of settling and developing millions of acres in the American West. But the act led to disputes between new and existing farmers who suddenly found themselves competing for land they hadn't bought because it had been government property. And there was also the little matter of the indigenous Native Americans who hadn't been told about any of this. The Homestead Acts are, in a way, the story of the American frontier and the settler experience in the latter half of the 19th century.

This is the background to and ultimately the cause of the conflict that draws Shane in. I have watched many Westerns with my children who love a good John Wayne flick and have had enough patience to sit through *Seven Samurai*, but they hated *Shane*, finding the young boy Joey utterly irritating. We never got to the final showdown and the famous ride off into the sunset (is he dead or not?), which is a shame because, on reflection, to the modern viewer that's definitely the best bit of the film.

Once again, we have a Western, often considered to be one of the most visually poetic of film genres, based on a book. The novel of the same name came out in 1949 and was written by Jack Schaefer. The motion picture is very similar to the novel and is a morally complex story. Shane has clearly been a bad man who is now hoping to turn his back on the past and begin anew. He starts by working for the Starrett family who give him the chance to rebuild himself into a better person, but a violent world isn't yet done with him, and he is forced to use the very skills he has been trying to leave behind. It turns out he is a better gunslinger than he is a farmhand, but at what cost? And does violence ever truly solve the problem?

For a book that came out just a few years after World War II, followed by a film not long after, there had to be more than a few men sitting in movie theatres reflecting on what they had done in the war versus their civilian lives after the war. Director George Stevens was one of those men. Stevens had already had a long and distinguished career (helping a young British comic called Stanley Laurel get a start in the industry). By the outbreak of the war, he had already directed a number of well-reviewed and commercially successful films, but he joined the US Army Signal Corps and was in Europe from 1943-46. He filmed the only existing colour footage of D-Day as well as the liberation of Paris and the liberation of Dachau, for which his footage was used as evidence in the Nuremberg trials. It is worth pointing out that during the war Hollywood stepped up not just by having stars like Jimmy Stewart put themselves in genuine peril, but also the directors, including Stevens, Ford and Frank Capra. In the case of Stevens, having seen the liberation of a concentration camp, he had witnessed firsthand man's inhumanity to man, and while it is conjecture, it's easy to deduce that the story of Shane's rejection of violence was one that Stevens wanted to tell. Stevens went the extra mile to show the consequences of violence. The sounds of gunfire are not stock sound effects but were specially recorded large calibre weapons being fired into a metal garbage can to make them sound almost deafening. He also had wires on the two men Shane guns down so that their hands would jerk with the imagined impact. This was a more graphic display of gun violence.

"There's no living with a killing" is Shane's parting line to the young Joey. It could be a summary of what many in the contemporary audiences had experienced and is still a powerful line today. Apparently, the filming of *Shane* had its tricky moments as the young actor playing Joey knew when the camera was on Ladd and kept sticking out his tongue trying to distract him.

Stevens was in his golden era when *Shane* was filmed. In 1952 he had won the Best Director Oscar for *A Place in the Sun*. He was nominated for *Shane* and would win again with *Giant* in 1957. Alan Ladd played Shane and he was the perfect choice. His heyday had been in the 40s, and his tough guy persona, a man who was now a little past his prime, fitted the character of Shane perfectly. The irony was that while Ladd may have projected a tough guy image, he hated guns. The scene where Shane demonstrates his shooting skills to the boy Joey took 116 takes, and the shootout in the saloon is nothing a John Wick film need worry about; Ladd looks stiff as a board and his gun isn't aimed anywhere near the men he is gunning down.

While the onset realities were complicated, that scene is not, especially compared to so many other movies of the time. The shootout is stark and simple, almost noir. The inside of the saloon is poorly lit and virtually empty. There is a little background music, but it is not intrusive, no wall of strings screeching to the finale; the tones are almost ambient in nature. When violence comes, it is fast, brutal, efficient. Watching the average Western of the day, gunfights looked like fun (it's why kids like to re-enact them in playground games), but this one is cold and dirty. Shane does it so that nobody else has to. It is, in short, a classic Hollywood scene.

It was with *Shane* that Paramount wanted to try out some new technology, so the film was shot in a new, flat widescreen format, which ushered in the era of the bigger the panorama, the more it was used. Was this an artistic choice? No, but Hollywood was fighting a new enemy, one that could dismantle its entire business model, television. Just as the movies crushed vaudeville and theatre, studio executives knew TV could do the same to the motion picture industry. (To all the live theatre aficionados, I am well aware that it still exists; it's just that 150 years ago everybody went, whereas nowadays, people don't usually finish work and then queue up to see *Les Misérables* or *Macbeth*.) Television could go out live and give viewers the news every day while news reels in movie theatres were shown once a week, which meant that much of the news was already a week old. However, cinema still had two big advantages: it was in colour and the screen was bigger, so if the studios made cuts in areas they had already lost but leant into the spectacles that TV couldn't match, motion pictures should be safe. It was no accident that the 50s saw the rise of the "sword-and-sandals" epics, featuring crowds of hundreds and reproductions of Ancient Rome on a scale that no TV broadcasters could hope to match. The Western genre was perfectly suited to help fight back against home viewing.

So, due to the use of new technology and the numerous takes, *Shane* was unusually expensive for what is a fairly modest story. The reviews were gushing and the film was a big box office hit that recouped the extra expense. With my sons' appraisals in mind, I would say that large tracts of the film are, by modern standards, dated, and there's no doubt that Joey is whiney and annoying. That said, the themes are important and timeless, and the last ten minutes are some of the greatest moments cinema has ever produced. *Shane* has seeped into pop culture, with references to it in other movies and TV shows. The film is so famous it is often used to signify that the person with knowledge about the film has a dark past but wants to make amends. There is an entire discussion about it in 1998's *The Negotiator*, and it gets a nod in 2017's *Logan*, a superhero movie that remodels Wolverine into a comic book version of *Shane* (the film is even playing in the background in one scene).

Another movie that has something morally complex to say is 1956's *The Searchers*. Again, like *Shane*, this is considered to be a crown jewel of the genre, if not of Hollywood as a whole. This film has one of the better representations of Native Americans in the 1950s. Although those playing the main members of the tribe are not First Nation people, but actors wearing toning makeup, the film does have a more nuanced view of Native Americans, and unusually for productions of the time, most of the extras were Navajos.

Many people are not aware that the film is based on real history. Throughout the 19th century, dozens of settler children were captured in raids carried out by Native Americans, a reminder that native tribes were capable of conducting acts of violence against civilians. The story in the movie bears close similarities to the abduction of nine-year-old Cynthia Ann Parker by Comanche warriors in 1836. She was to spend twenty-four years with the Comanches and eventually married a chief with whom she had three children. In 1860, the tribe was attacked by Texas Rangers who returned her to her family against her will. During the time of her capture, Cynthia Ann's uncle devoted his time and fortune trying to find his niece. This is basically the plot of the film.

The obsessive hunt is conducted by John Wayne as Ethan, a man so hell-bent on finding his niece Debbie and returning her to her home that he becomes a cold-blooded racist in the process, and by the end of the film, he is just as savage and violent as the men who kidnapped her. Like *Shane*, the movie is famous for its final scene where everyone gathers inside the house, everyone except Ethan who, framed by the doorway, a bright light behind him, turns away from the homestead. He is a man of the Old West, and he no longer belongs inside with a civilised family.

We know Ford could be a bully, but he had a soft side to him as well. Harry Carey was an actor mentioned earlier who had already done some silent films with Ford but who had died in 1947. In *The Searchers* Ford cast Carey's widow, Olive Carey, as Mrs. Jorgensen, the girl's mother, and Carey's son, Harry Carey Jr, as Brad, one of the sons, as a tribute to the actor. In the closing scene where we see Ethan framed in the doorway, Wayne does something odd. He holds his right elbow with his left hand in a way that looks like it's been injured. Although a deliberate pose to reflect an often-seen Carey gesture, it was not a pose Harry Carey fans would necessarily recognise. Wayne later stated he did it as a tribute to the actor while, off-camera, Olive Carey watched.

The Searchers gives us an imperfect view of Native American life, but it was a step in the right direction, and Wayne's performance was his most nuanced to date. Levity is created with Ethan's sidekick Martin, played by Jeffrey Hunter, who at one point thinks he is negotiating for goods only to discover that he has unwittingly married a young Native American girl. The adult Debbie was played by Natalie Wood, who was still in high school at the time of filming. Occasionally John Wayne would pick her up from school to go to the set, which, of course, made her the envy of the entire school.

Today, the role of a Native American woman would have been played by someone of that ethnicity. Natalie Wood was of Ukrainian/Russian ancestry, so geographically speaking, about as far removed as you can get from the American West. She was in a similar situation playing the Puerto Rican Maria in *West Side Story*. She had come to Hollywood's attention with her breakout role a year earlier playing Judy in *Rebel Without a Cause*. Her appearance in major movies at such a young age was an indication of her formidable acting talent, but she had grown up on film sets, having appeared on TV and in the movies from the age of five. Her suspicious drowning in 1981 ended a career that had been going on for more than thirty-five years, and yet she was dead at only forty-three.

While modern audiences are uncomfortable with simplistic racial stereotypes, it's worth noting that while making the film, one of the extras, a Navajo (not Comanche) child, became seriously ill and needed urgent medical attention. John Wayne had his private airplane on location and had his pilot take the girl to hospital; she lived thanks to the rapid medical response to her pneumonia. Because of this the Navajos on the set named Wayne "The Man with the Big Eagle".

The Searchers was innovative in two ways: it was one of the first films to be shot in the new VistaVision widescreen format; the other innovation had to do with the PR around the film. Warner Bros produced and broadcast one of the first behind-the-scenes, "making-of" programmes in movie history. Today such footage is commonplace, but for audiences in the 50s, this was something new and a sign of the confidence Warner

Bros had in the movie. This behind-the-scenes footage was aired as an episode of the *Warner Bros Presents* TV series.

The film isn't set on the Utah/Arizona borders, but that didn't stop Ford shooting at Monument Valley … again. This led to a contemporary criticism of the film that while Ethan goes on a journey that lasts for years, because the background scenery is so samey throughout, it doesn't look like he's travelled very far. Another criticism concerns Ethan's motivation; his obsession with finding a member of his extended member family is hard to understand and would make more sense if he was trying to find his own daughter. The conundrum is resolved in the movie when, at the start, just before the raid on the homestead, we see the tombstone of Ethan's mother when Debbie hides next to it. The epitaph reveals the source of Ethan's glaring hatred for Comanches and reads: "Here lies Mary Jane Edwards killed by Comanches May 12, 1852. A good wife and mother in her 41st year." In other words, the Comanches have caused Ethan nothing but pain his whole life.

The "making of" was never meant to be a warts-and-all piece of cinema verité. It was a puff piece, designed to raise interest. Filming in the desert had its hazards and did nothing to help Ford's mood; he was his usual aggressive and irritable self throughout. When he was stung by a scorpion, C V Whitney, a major financial backer of this expensive movie was worried about the consequences if the director died, so he asked Wayne, "What if we lose him? What are we going to do?" Wayne offered to check on the director and returned from Ford's trailer, saying, "It's okay. John's fine, it's the scorpion that died". Unsurprisingly, this exchange didn't make it into the TV special.

The Searchers came out to strong reviews. Look magazine summarised the tone by describing it as a "Homeric odyssey". The idea of the arduous journey beset by perils as a man tries to achieve an obsessive goal is a pretty good comparison. While Wayne as Ethan is the man we follow throughout the film, he is not the stereotypical good guy; the era of the white-hat-wearing Tom Mix was long gone. Ethan is an obsessive, a man who sees the natives as savages; the film tells his story but does not agree with his perspective. Looking back at the previous chapter, Wayne's journey started in 1948's *Red River* when Ford recognised the actor could do more than just be a sentient hat. In *The Searchers* we have a morally ambiguous man who is more of a cautionary tale than a hero.

The film was a Wayne and Ford picture, so it was a big hit. This is an example of a movie that since its initial release has not only survived the hype, but as each new generation of critics assesses it, has eclipsed it as the reviews grow loftier and loftier. Ford was trying to say something, but he was also trying to entertain. Is this the closest the Western has come to Shakespeare? The bard is lauded by the intelligentsia, but in reality, during his lifetime, he just wanted to fill a theatre and have people leave with big smiles on their faces because they had been thoroughly entertained. This is another Western preserved in the Library of Congress.

After such gritty films, let's take a look at 1955's *Oklahoma!* The film was based on the 1943 theatre musical of the same name by Rodgers and Hammerstein, which was based on the non-musical play from 1931, *Green Grow the Lilacs*. Like all good musicals, it's essentially a love story. It has no great consequences, nations will not fall, nobody is on a bloody quest for revenge. It's boy meets girl and the two of them sing in each other's faces.

This Western musical originated a distribution trend. It was the first of the huge roadshow musical films to open in a limited number of theatres before its general release. The practice was called "reserved seat engagement" and created a buzz of anticipation while also mimicking the excitement of seeing a live performance available only in the theatre. So, while 1969's *Hello Dolly!* at first shared only an exclamation mark with *Oklahoma!*, the distribution plan for that film was simply following the plan that certainly had a role in the success of *Oklahoma!* which had come out nearly fifteen years earlier.

Oklahoma! is packed full of classic tunes, from the title song to "Oh, What a Beautiful Mornin'" a personal favourite, "The Surrey with the Fringe on the Top" and the lewd for the times, "I Cain't (sic) Say No". In fact, the relatively tame stage versions of the songs had to be edited for sexual inuendo in order to pass Hays Code scrutiny, so the code was stricter than Broadway.

The rights to the stage play were bought for a then record $1 million, the cost of an entire Western film of the age - and then they had to make it. Ironically, because the modern Oklahoma was so peppered with oil wells, location filming was shot in Arizona. It was an expensive production that already had a million-dollar starting cost, so while it did great business at the box office, overall, it didn't initially make money. But it won two Oscars and the re-releases and ancillary earnings made it a nice money spinner for the studio.

In the same year as *The Searchers* there was another classic that has become well regarded over the decades, *Giant*. George Stevens directed Elizabeth Taylor, Rock Hudson and James Dean, and in 1956, stars didn't come any bigger than these (plus there was a young Dennis Hopper in the background, but he would become a bigger deal a decade later).

Giant was based on Edna Ferber's book of the same name; she had also written Cimarron, and like that novel/movie, *Giant* is an epic sweep of ranchers' lives. This is no simple outlaw/gunman tale, and once again, as with *Cimarron*, it breaks the Western timeframe and signifiers as outlined by Frank Gruber. Set in the 1920s, the film is a mixture of social commentary and good, old-fashioned love triangle. In her role as Leslie, Taylor is new to ranch life and is appalled by the second-class status of women, something she has not previously experienced, and it chafes. In addition, she sees the working conditions of the Hispanic labourers as despicable and tries to convince Hudson (the owner and patriarch of the ranch) to do something about it. Taylor marries Hudson but is pursued by the ranch hand Dean (although history tells us it was more likely that Hudson and Dean would get together).

This 1956 movie has more in common with *Killers of the Flower Moon* from 2023 than *The Searchers*. It's the first example (in terms of chronological time) of a Western set in the era of the automobile. This type of vehicular Western will return in later chapters, but *Giant* is a prescient bridge spanning the decades between *Cimarron* and the more modern Westerns with oilfields and pickup trucks as portrayed in TV shows like *Dallas* (*Giant* is set in the oilfields of Texas) or *Yellowstone*. The drama doesn't come from shootouts but from affairs of the heart and business deals where livelihoods could be destroyed.

Filming was equally epic. The budget was almost double that of *The Searchers*, making it one of the most expensive films of the day. But the money is up there onscreen, with sweeping panoramic shots, including aerial photography of huge cattle drives. The movie was meant to induce people to see it in cinemas rather than squinting at it on a black and white TV a year later on CBS. Filming was split between location shooting in Texas and studio work in California. When the production moved to Texas, the Victorian mansion set filled multiple train carriages. The location filming was near the tiny town of Marfa and took two months. Unusually, it was not a closed set as Stevens needed the ranch to look busy, so curious local residents who came to the site were often used as extras.

Grace Kelly and Elizabeth Taylor were both under consideration for the role of Leslie. Stevens couldn't decide so asked Hudson who he would choose. Hudson said he preferred Taylor, and they got on very well during the shoot, becoming lifelong friends. During filming, Taylor took the young James Dean under her wing. He was having a tough time adjusting to life as a movie star, and she empathised, having been in the limelight from childhood. Hudson and Dean, however, did not get on. Dean was from a new school of acting, and the two men clashed on approaches to their roles but also, allegedly, because Dean rebuffed Hudson's advances.

One of Dean's coping mechanisms for dealing with fame included racing cars. When Director Stevens found out, he was afraid his young star might come to harm and instructed Dean not to do it again until after shooting. There were also many times when Dean was late, although Stevens recognised that this was usually because he was getting into character. Meanwhile, Taylor and her then husband Michael Wilding invited Rock Hudson and his future wife to their house for get-to-know-you drinks at the start of the production. (In the 1950s, a leading man could not be openly gay without a backlash, so Hudson lived a lie for most of his life. It's a credit to his acting ability that he was able to play a convincing heterosexual love interest both on and off screen for decades.) Hudson described it as a "liquid evening"; they all got wasted and the "evening" finished at 3:00 a.m. Taylor's call-time was 5:30 a.m., and Hudson's wasn't long after that. Fortunately, the scene being shot that morning was a wedding scene with no dialogue, so all they had to do was look lovingly at each other. Hudson and Taylor were concentrating so hard on not throwing up that they were quite surprised when some of the people on the set started to cry, so convinced were they of their supposed looks of adoration at each other.

Giant was Stevens' next project after *Shane*, but it didn't come out until three years later for two reasons: First and foremost, Stevens was a meticulous editor and spent more than a year putting the film together. Secondly, and tragically, Dean died in a car crash just a week after shooting had finished, meaning that someone else had to be brought in to dub over some scenes. Dean was just twenty-four at the time of his death.

After a lengthy production and a lot of money, Warner Bros won big. Not only did *Giant* come out to great reviews and win George Stevens another Oscar, but it was a mega box office hit. It was Warner Bros' biggest grossing movie of all time until 1978's *Superman*.

Then in 1958, there was *The Big Country* with Gregory Peck, Jean Simmons and Charlton Heston. The setup is an ex-sea captain comes home to help on the ranch. There are rivalries, horses, duels - and two young people from the warring families who fall for each other. Director William Wyler was known for shooting take after take on his films, something Stanley Kubrick would become notorious for, but unlike Kubrick, Wyler would do it without explaining to the actors what to do differently except "make it better". Filming was a nightmare. Jean Simmons was so traumatised by the experience that she refused to talk about it for years until an interview in the 1980s when she revealed,

"We'd have our lines learned, then receive a rewrite, stay up all night learning the new version, then receive yet another rewrite the following morning. It made the acting damned near impossible".

The result was a movie that got mixed reviews but did well at the box office. So, why is a movie of such unexceptional quality in the book? Because of its music; except for full-blown musicals, this is the one feature that has not so far been mentioned. *The Big Country* came out in the middle of the classic era of the Western, with big shootouts, big characters and big hats. But the one thing that has yet to be discussed is the musical score. *The Searchers* is a perfect movie, but can you hum the theme tune? The theme of *The Big Country* by Jerome Moross is the definitive classic Western piece of music, and every musical instrument in it is contemporary to the time portrayed onscreen, so, violins, trumpets and so on. But as there's no music hall and no full orchestra within a thousand miles of the ranch, the music is clearly coming from a different place. This was a Western first and it worked! The music, with its sweeping strings and brash trumpets creates the right mood and enhances whatever scenes are playing out onscreen; it is euphoric and everything you'd expect to hear as a man gallops over the prairie. It is impossible to convey this in writing, so bookmark this page and go to YouTube and listen to it, then you'll see what I mean. This rather average movie inspired the definitive Western score. We will be returning later to musical scores to discuss another piece of music that's even more definitely Western than this, but for the classic era, *The Big Country* theme is the best part of the movie. Quite simply, it is just over three minutes of perfection.

Filmed in 1958 but out in 1959 was *Rio Bravo*, a Howard Hawks and John Wayne classic that, while based on a short story, was conceived as a rebuttal to *High Noon*. As previously mentioned, Wayne not only didn't like the film but thought it was fundamentally "un-American". Hawks agreed with Wayne stating, "I didn't think a good sheriff was going to go running around town like a chicken with his head cut off, asking for help, and finally his Quaker wife had to save him". They also had a problem with the townsfolk leaving the sheriff completely on his own; they didn't pull together, you know, like a community, just like good, God fearing, anti-communist, Americans would do.

The point that both director and star were trying to make pushed them to create a movie regarded as one of both men's best-ever work. The story is nice and simple: the brother of a notorious outlaw has been captured, and the small-town sheriff (played by Wayne) enlists the help of a disabled man, a drunk, and a young gunfighter in his efforts to hold the brother in jail. The film has a tense, siege-like quality to it. The drunk, called Dude, is played to perfection by Dean Martin, and the old lame guy helps out by exchanging shots in the gunfights and even throwing dynamite. So, even the less able members of the local community were eager and able to help the sheriff thwart the outlaws. *Rio Bravo* has explosions, shootouts and even some comedy (courtesy of Dean Martin). It is everything you want from a John Wayne film. Unusually, he even gets the girl at the end.

The young gunslinger is played by Ricky Nelson, an up-and-coming singer in the 50s, so with him and Dean Martin in the cast, opportunities were created for both to sing either in the film or on the soundtrack, something not previously seen in a John Wayne movie. But the movie was a hit and the soundtrack sold well. Critically, it was recognised for what it was, a fun romp of a film; this was not *The Searchers*, but it wasn't trying to be. The goal was to entertain, and it did. Both Wayne and Hawks clearly enjoyed making it because they were to remake it twice, both times with Wayne as the Sheriff, in 1966 as *El Dorado* and again in 1970, as *Rio Lobo*. I grew up with *El Dorado* and loved the gags around the young James Caan, who was great with a knife but a bad shot, so they give him a double-barrelled, sawn-off shotgun. But in amongst the fun parts, there is a sequence of the most racist stereotypes of Chinese culture which I had forgotten about and led me to fast-forwarding when I showed it to my children. The other thing I noticed when watching it years later was that the background score was strangely reminiscent of something else. I checked and there's a reason for that: the composer

Nelson Riddle worked on both *El Dorado* and the Adam West Batman series in 1966. The result was musical scores that noticeably resemble each other, and it was more than a little odd watching a John Wayne character in the Old West acting against a musical background similar to that of Batman talking to the Joker.

The idea of a jail surrounded by the enemy and the officers of law enforcement having to ally with the prisoners so that everyone can stay alive was brought into the modern world in 1976 when John Carpenter turned it into *Assault on Precinct 13*, a film that was itself remade in 2005. So that is five films created because John Wayne and Howard Hawks didn't like *High Noon*.

After the cottage industry that was *Rio Bravo*, we come to another passion project of John Wayne's, *The Alamo*. The Battle of the Alamo is seared not only into the consciousness of every proud Texan, but until the early 21st century was a moment in American history that was taught in every American school (the events got another movie in 2004). The story of the Alamo was the pivotal event of the Texas Revolution. Alamo Mission, near San Antonio, was surrounded by President General Antonio López de Santa Anna with 2,000 soldiers of the Mexican army. Inside the compound was a mixture of freebooters, adventurers and explorers numbering about 200. The odds were impossibly stacked against them, but it still took thirteen days for Santa Anna to break in and kill virtually all the defenders. Santa Anna's refusal to take prisoners during the battle inspired many Texians and Tejanos to join the Texian Army. Because Texas was still technically part of Mexico at this time, this was not regarded as a fight between the US Army and Mexico. Motivated by a desire for revenge, the Texians defeated the Mexican Army at the Battle of San Jacinto a month after the Alamo fell in April 1836. This defeat ended attempts by the Mexicans to retain control of the territory that became the new Republic of Texas.

Some of the Alamo's defenders were legendary at the time and only became more so afterwards. There was James Bowie of Bowie knife fame and Davy Crockett, "King of the Wild Frontier", with the racoon skin hat named after him. Wayne first had the idea for the film in 1945, but it took three years to research the history and get a screenplay together with Patrick Ford (John Ford's son). When legal wranglings ensued, Wayne was back to square one but still determined to make his vision of this very American martyrdom. He only officially directed two movies in his career, this one and *The Green Berets* (there are another uncredited three), but the two films that have his face slapped on the posters and his name highlighted as the director are incredibly jingoistic. Initially, he didn't even want to appear as an actor in *The Alamo*, but when he was asking for millions of dollars for its budget, it was only prudent to get "The Duke" in front of the cameras. So, Wayne took on the role of Davy Crockett. He sank $1.5 million of his own money in the project, even though it meant raising a second mortgage on his home.

The reconstruction of the Alamo was not a plywood set but was made of genuine adobe stone and took two years to construct. Fourteen miles of paved roads were laid along with miles of sewage and water lines. Engineers sank six wells to provide 12,000 gallons of water each day and they also built 5,000 acres of horse corrals. Before filming had even begun the production was costing a small fortune. The infrastructure and set were so good, they were used for years afterwards in other movies. Filming *The Alamo* lasted three months, extras were hired in their hundreds, and the budget soared to a massive $12 million.

This was all extremely impressive, but was it a Western? It's outside of Frank Gruber's dates, and as it centres on a siege, is it really a war movie? Technically, the events don't even take place in the United States. But we have John Wayne surrounded by the enemy, firing guns, and talking about freedom, so it certainly has elements of the myths around the making of the Old West, and the siege of the Alamo was an instrumental moment in the expansion westwards of the United States of America.

The project was incredibly personal to Wayne as the film pauses (way too many times) while almost any and all characters talk about their love of freedom, which can be summarised in one speech by

Wayne: "Republic. I like the sound of the word. Means that people can live free, talk free, go or come, buy or sell, be drunk or sober, however they choose. Some words give you a feeling. Republic is one of those words that makes me tight in the throat." The sincerity of his words is obvious, but when all the careful research conducted by the two historical advisors was largely ignored, they asked to have their names removed from the credits. Despite the three-hour, thirteen-minute runtime, the movie does very little to put the events in context, and virtually all the exchanges were made up. It was a huge box office success, but it was not big enough to cover the eye-watering costs, and Wayne was forced to sell the rights to recoup his losses. *The Alamo* did, however, win an Oscar ... for Best Sound. After this financial disaster, it was somewhat surprising that Disney had a go at the battle again in 2004, and it was again called, quite simply, *The Alamo*. With all due respect to the talents of Dennis Quaid and Billy Bob Thornton, neither had had the same box office success as John Wayne. And despite the warnings that the excessive budget would make it hard to recoup the costs, Disney, for some unknown reason, gave the film a $107 million budget plus marketing expenses. The film grossed less than a quarter of the original budget, leading to total losses of around $146 million. This makes John Wayne's efforts look smart by comparison.

At the start of the book, I compared the mythmaking of the Old West to that around the samurais of Japan. This was not an accident because while these films were being made in the West, samurai films were being made in the East. And arguably the greatest Japanese director of all time, Akira Kurosawa, would be drawn to the story of the samurai. Kurosawa originally wanted to be a painter, which is a telling influence in his much later colour samurai epics *Kagemusha* (1980) and *Ran* (1985). In 1948, he made *Drunken Angel*, a contemporary Yakuza film starring the then little-known Toshiro Mifune. The two would go on to collaborate a further fifteen times, including on some of the greatest movies ever made, and three are in this book because these samurai films were repurposed into Westerns. This may sound odd, but the idea of a lone warrior wandering into town, righting wrongs and getting into tense battles is exactly what a good Western is made of. And this is ironic as Kurosawa himself was influenced by films from the West, including ones about cowboys. Indeed, some of his contemporary critics thought his films weren't Japanese enough. So, we have Westerns influencing samurai films, which go on to influence Westerns.

In 1950, Kurosawa created his international calling card *Rashomon*. It's rare for a filmmaker to create an entirely new narrative technique, but Kurosawa did it here. In the film, some peasants find a dead samurai and go to the authorities to tell them what they discovered. The problem occurs when a bandit (Mifune) is captured, and he tells a different story, and at the end, there are multiple versions of the same event. As the truth cannot be definitively known, the audience is left to decide which version of these contradictory accounts is, on balance, the correct one. It is an ingenious idea, not least because it virtually demands a rewatch in the cinema. Once this new plot took hold, it was often repeated even as recently as Ridley Scott's *The Last Duel* from 2021, more than seventy years later.

The idea was so good that *Rashomon* was turned into two Westerns. *Valerie* from 1957, starring Sterling Hayden and Anita Ekberg, was a very average affair, inferior in every possible way to the original. In 1964, Hollywood tried it again with *The Outrage*, starring Paul Newman and William Shatner. It's a bit better than *Valerie* but not by much, and neither will be worrying the Library of Congress. However, the idea of using stories from samurai movies was now in play and would be done much better with one of Kurosawa's masterpieces.

In 1954, Kurosawa made *Seven Samurai*, the most expensive Japanese movie ever made up to that point. It is often cited as the first true action movie (where the actions of characters tell the audience about their personalities and motivations). It was also the first film to assemble a team to carry out a specific mission. How many heist movies spend half their runtime gathering the team, or how many war movies get the unit together and then go over the plan that leads to the final set piece.

It's a straightforward story: poor peasant farmers are being harassed by bandits, so they go to town and hire a samurai to teach them how to defend themselves. In the end, the samurai brings six others onboard and they, with some help from the villagers, fight off and eventually defeat the bandits. Change the word samurai to gunslinger and you have another story ripe for a remake set on the western frontier. I feel obliged to add (and this is a great pub quiz question) that the samurai, like knights, come from a feudal tradition, and like knights, they must have a master. The height of embarrassment according to Bushido (the chivalric code of samurai) is for a samurai to lose his master, in which case they are now leaderless and are known as ronin. The samurai in the film have no masters, so the film should technically be The Seven Ronin; the irony is that there are no samurai in this classic samurai movie. *Seven Samurai* had near perfect reviews not just at the time of release, but decades later. The film was a huge hit both in Japan and internationally and more than recovered its costs. Seventy years later, it is the BFI's bestselling home media title.

So, unsurprisingly, *Seven Samurai* received the Hollywood remake treatment with 1960's *The Magnificent Seven,* but unlike *Valerie* or *The Outrage*, a lot of time, effort and star power was put into the movie. Yul Brynner starred and Steve McQueen was right there behind him. As well as this film, Charles Bronson was in *The Great Escape* and *The Dirty Dozen,* the three famous "group" movies of the 60s. (Another pub quiz fact: Bronson managed to survive or escape in all three movies.) Robert Vaughn and James Coburn were the next level of stardom and the rest of the seven were made up by the capable supporting cast of Horst Buchholz and Brad Dexter.

Eli Wallach played Calvera, the leader of the bandits in what feels like an origin story for Tuco in *The Good, the Bad and the Ugly*. It was a great ensemble cast where McQueen turned out to be a bigger presence than the script indicated. Brynner was the big name star of the film, but watch the movie again, and it becomes obvious that McQueen would eclipse Brynner's stardom. There are multiple scenes where McQueen's character says nothing, but McQueen understood that cinema is a visual medium, and so he is forever loading his gun, or playing with his hat, or scouring the distance for bandits. His movements draw the eye to him, not Brynner, thus making his part bigger than it was intended to be. Like *Seven Samurai*, every member of the group has something that singles them out: Coburn is the guy who is good with knives as seen in a duel he is reluctant to participate in because he has no interest in killing the man (just like the master swordsman in the original). Vaughn's role as Lee is an interesting character study of a man with a fearsome reputation who has lost his appetite for violence and is now useless in a gunfight.

Directed by John Sturges, the movie was almost as ambitious a project as the original. The village and the town were scratch built in Mexico. There were tensions on set with such a large ensemble cast. Elmer Bernstein wrote the score and gives the film a theme that fills the listener with images of the epic nature of the wild frontier (personal opinion: it's number two only to the theme of *The Big Country*). Years later, Sturges met Kurosawa, who told him that he loved *The Magnificent Seven*. Sturges considered this to be the proudest moment of his professional career.

The Magnificent Seven, while well reviewed (but not a critical darling), was not initially a box office hit in America. However, the rest of the world loved it, and its international release enabled the movie to turn a profit. This is a reminder that Americana has always been popular with the rest of the world. Other countries have horses and guns, but it's that combination along with the music, the scenery and the hats that are of endless appeal. Today *The Magnificent Seven* is regarded as one of the greatest Westerns ever made. Not bad for a story originally set in 1500s Japan.

Yul Brynner was the only member of the original cast to return for the sequel *Return of the Seven - but even* he didn't come back for number three, *Guns of the Magnificent Seven*. And on into the 1970s there was *The Magnificent Seven Ride!* None of them were as successful critically, commercially or in terms of legacy as the original. There have been many unofficial remakes, including 1980's sci-fi version *Battle Beyond the Stars*, a cheap *Star Wars* knockoff that had Robert Vaughn back in the team. The number of remakes, official or otherwise, of the original *Seven Samurai* concept are too long to list. The Western version did get a straight remake in 2016 starring Denzel Washington and Chris Pratt.

The apogee of this East/West crossover is the veritable UN of movies, 1971's *Red Sun*. The story is set in the 1870s when a Japanese diplomatic mission is held up and robbed by bandits in the Wild West. The Japanese reluctantly hand over a golden katana, meant to be a gift for the President. When the lead robber is double-crossed, he begrudgingly teams up with the samurai to get it back. The samurai is played by cinema's most legendary samurai, Toshiro Mifune, the robber is played by Charles Bronson. Coincidence number one: Mifune was in *The Seven Samurai*, Bronson was in *The Magnificent Seven*, the cowboy retelling of the story. Coincidence number two: The double-crossing robber is played by French heartthrob Alain Delon who, in 1967, starred as an assassin in *Le Samourai*. The film was directed by the Brit, Terence Young, who had directed a number of James Bond films, including *Dr No*, which connects him to the Swiss movie star Ursula Andress, who plays Delon's love interest in *Red Sun*.

Filmed in Spain, there are comical culture clashes, double-crosses that lead to eventual mutual respect and gun/sword fights with bandits and natives. Want to know who would win the fight between an indigenous warrior and a samurai? This movie has the answer. The exotic mix of nationalities and cultures add a sense of novelty to what is, under the fresh coat of paint, a very standard western.

And so we come to the year 1969, the tail end of the classic Western, and therefore, the closing stage of this chapter. By this time there were signs that things were changing, and while a new generation demanded something different from the Western genre, it can take Hollywood a while to notice things. So to conclude the era of the classic Western, let's take a look at a complete failure and a final hurrah. Let's start with the disaster.

By 1969, Lee Marvin and Clint Eastwood (this is Clint's first mention, but he will be prominent in several chapters to come) had been playing cowboys for years. Everyone recognised them in their brimmed hats with guns on their hips. But the question nobody had asked was, can they sing? Well, good news, *Paint Your Wagon* had the answer. This rip roarin', slap stick musical extravaganza was a terrible idea; it was completely miscast and had more money thrown at it than King Solomon had in his mines. *Paint Your Wagon* was Paramount's panic writ large. TV was taking viewers away, so the proposed solution was to give audiences SPECTACLE, to fill their eyeballs with visuals the cathode ray tube at home couldn't deliver. Competition was also coming from the bloodier, grittier, lower budget foreign and independent movies being produced, but they were mucky and not family friendly, so the idea was to counter them with good, clean family fun, and nothing says family fun like a musical comedy.

While both Marvin and Eastwood had climbed the greasy pole of stardom in the late 50s and early 60s, they had done this as tough guys. Neither were trained singers and neither came from any musical tradition. In fact, both had military backgrounds. Marvin had been a marine, wounded in World War II; Eastwood had served as a swimming instructor in the army during the Korean War. The obvious unease of both men in the film is there to see. Eastwood sings "I Talk to the Trees" unconvincingly, and Marvin singing "Wand'rin' Star" hits notes so low they barely register in human hearing and must have caused seismic activity in the region.

The film was not the creation of a studio exec's fever dream but started off via the usual route of adapting an existing work, in this case, Alan Jay Lerner's successful Broadway musical Paint Your Wagon. The problem wasn't the musical, it was literally everything else. The set cost $2.4 million, a rainstorm washed away the only road to the site and that had to be rebuilt at a cost of $10,000 per mile. Marvin got a cool million to star and Eastwood wasn't far behind with $750,000. Their combined salaries were the cost of the average Western at the time. My favourite story from the set and a great metaphor for an older generation clashing with a younger one, concerns the groups of hippies hired as extras. They resented the low pay, unionised and collectively got a raise. The already approved budget spiralled out of control and doubled to $20 million. But the film was made, and the final release came in at two hours forty-four minutes - the typical length of a Broadway musical but way too long for a film like this.

It is not fair to say that it was a critical and commercial disaster. Reviews were mixed rather than scathing, but for a mega-budgeted studio behemoth, that was not a good sign. The film did well for Paramount at the box office, but because of eyewatering budgetary and marketing expenses it did not turn a profit. Today it is regarded as a curiosity; nobody is going to say *Paint Your Wagon* is either a classic musical or Western. It was, in fact, one of the last hurrahs of the studio system, a vivid embodiment of the end of days with its cracks all too apparent. But there was a bizarre silver lining to this film and Lee Marvin's career. In 1970, when songs like "Suspicious Minds" by Elvis or "I Want You Back" by the Jackson Five were hitting the top of the music charts, "Wand'rin' Star" made it to number one in the UK (and that is my favourite fact in the whole book).

Meanwhile, while Paramount was fumbling around cluelessly with their Western, The Duke was reminding everyone how to do it right. Sensibly budgeted, *True Grit* delivered what the film was meant to deliver: a good story in classic Western mode, well-acted and well told. It grossed slightly less than *Paint Your Wagon* at the box office, but unlike that film, it turned a nice profit for the studio and garnered excellent reviews.

True Grit is a slightly bleak exploration of the concept of the US Marshal, a branch of American law enforcement that still exists today and is unique in that there are no meaningful equivalents in other countries. In the 19th century they were the main source of day-to-day law enforcement in areas that had no local police. It was the US Marshals, as opposed to local sheriffs, who were key to enforcing law and order in the Wild West, and they spent most of their time hunting down outlaws and troublemakers. Those "Wanted" posters, were real, and the price on a wanted man's head ("dead or alive") was called a bounty, so the people who made it their job to find these criminals were known as bounty hunters. However, if a US Marshal got them first, well, that was their job so no reward for them. Although marshals today are required to have bachelor's degrees and police experience, things were a lot less formal in the 1800s, and some marshals were reformed criminals. They were tough men who brought tough justice to the frontiers.

In *True Grit* John Wayne plays US Marshal Rooster Cogburn, an over-the-hill, often drunk, one-eyed marshal known for his "true grit". He always gets his man and is prone to excessive force, usually bringing them in dead. He is hired by a teenage girl Mattie Ross (played by Kim Darby), who wants him to catch her father's killers so they can face justice. The film came out thirty years after *Stagecoach* and Wayne, now in his 60s, is no Ringo Kid. What we see here is a man with a past, a grittier version of his earlier *Stagecoach* character. Cogburn is no father figure, and he resents the girl because she rebukes him, argues with him and will not stand for his complaints. She has heard he has true grit and she wants to see it!

Wayne is completely believable as a man who has been in the saddle for decades because he was; he was an excellent rider because it was his job. He would play the Cogburn role again in 1975's *Rooster Cogburn*. This time the bickering was not between Wayne and a girl, but between Wayne and another member of the Hollywood aristocracy, Katharine Hepburn. The two of them were clearly having the time of their lives making the film, and it did good business, but both the film and the box office takings of the sequel pale in comparison with the original.

True Grit was remade in 2010 and starred Jeff Bridges who played Cogburn as even more slovenly to the point of being borderline incomprehensible. Bridges does a great job, but it's a thankless task trying to emulate John Wayne in one of his signature roles. The Cohen brothers breathed new life into the plot, and the whole thing has the air of a quality remake rather than a cheap Hollywood cash grab. It's better than the sequel, but as technically good as the remake is, there's no John Wayne in it.

While the music is from the classic era, and the hero is from the classic era, there are signs of change. The tone is far more downbeat, more *A Fistful of Dollars* than *Fort Apache*. The main outlaw is played by Robert Duvall, soon to appear in *The Godfather,* and one of the main henchmen is Dennis Hopper appearing here in the same year *Easy Rider* came out. The final exchange between Duvall and Wayne before the climactic shootout could almost be an exchange between the two eras of the Western:

> Wayne: I mean to kill you in one minute, Ned. Or see you hanged in Fort Smith at Judge Parker's convenience. Which'll it be?
>
> Duvall: I call that bold talk for a one-eyed fat man.
>
> Wayne: Fill your hand, you son of a bitch!

And with that, Wayne finally wins the Best Actor Oscar in 1970. When Barbra Streisand announced his name, there was a huge cheer from the crowd as a Hollywood legend, past his prime, finally received the much-deserved recognition for a decades-long career. And he had to beat John Voight, Richard Burton, Peter O'Toole and Dustin Hoffmann, the new generation of leading men to win it. He walked up to the stage, the hard man of everyone's childhood, wiped away a tear and said, "Wow! If I'd I known that I would have put that patch on thirty-five years earlier."

Chapter 4

Code Red

Throughout the last two chapters there can be no doubt that the most common name mentioned is that of John Wayne. There is a reason for that. Born in 1907, he was of a different generation to that of other stars. By the time he made *True Grit* he was getting close to retirement age. Clint Eastwood only makes a brief cameo appearance at the end of the previous chapter because being born in 1930 meant his career as a cowboy coincided with a major change in the film industry and audience expectations.

At this point we need to look again at the Hays Code which guaranteed there was nothing too strong in content so that the whole family could go to see the same films. It had been introduced in 1934, but by the early 60s things were starting to change. This was in no small part due to foreign films and not just foreign language films, but also British films that were not restricted by the American code. The rest of the world's cinema was maturing, America's was not. Art house movies became popular because they showed movies of moral complexity from France, scenes of nudity from Italy and more graphic violence from Japan. In 1963, the President of the MPAA (Motion Picture Association of America, now more commonly known as the MPA, the organisation in charge of the Hays Code) Eric Johnston died. He had been slowly adjusting the code as audience attitudes changed, and there followed a power struggle between those who wanted to remain conservative and stick to the code and the liberals who wanted to further loosen it. After three years the liberals won, but the result was a lack of clear guidance and a loosening of restrictions. Perhaps the most famous MPAA nonapproved film during this time was *Some Like It Hot*. But once the genie was out of the bottle there was no realistic way to put it back in.

The MPAA began to start thinking about a ratings system so people would know if the movie was more suitable for children or adults. In 1966, Warner Bros released *Who's Afraid of Virginia Woolf?*, the first film to come with a pseudo rating "Suggested for Mature Audiences" (SMA). The film received Production Code approval despite previously prohibited language. The original code (see chapter 2) was replaced by a list of eleven points outlining that the boundaries of the new code would be defined by current community standards and good taste. Any film containing content deemed suitable for older audiences would feature the SMA label in its advertising. With the creation of this new rating, the MPAA began classifying films, a job it still does today.

The SMA label was refined in 1968 to four rating symbols: "G" was for general exhibition (persons of all ages), "M" was for mature audiences, "R" meant it was restricted (persons under 16 not admitted unless accompanied by a parent or adult guardian), and "X" meant persons under 16 would not be admitted. This closely linked to the modern American rating system, where G is still G, M is PG, R is still R and X is now NC-17. The only addition was PG-13 after Steven Spielberg's stronger family movies *Indiana Jones and the Temple of Doom* and *Gremlins* (the first he directed, the second he produced) in 1984. These family movies featured more intense scenes than other films, but they clearly weren't aimed at an adult market, so at the time both got a PG rating by the skin of their teeth. However, Spielberg suggested a stronger family rating which became PG-13. The first film to be awarded the rating was 1985's *Red Dawn*.

With the decline of the Hays Code and the introduction of the rating system, combined with the looser restrictions on motion pictures made outside of America, the 60s saw the rise of a new kind of Western, a tougher, more violent Western with greater moral ambiguity and blood, lots and lots of blood.

The first of this new type of Western to get into trouble with the MPAA were those that became known as Spaghetti Westerns. The name is highly misleading as many of the famous ones were filmed in Spain. Some of the famous directors were Italian, but with Americans cast in the main roles and the rest of the cast dubbed Spaniards, maybe the best name for these movies is UN Westerns.

The first one is a forgotten film from 1961 called *The Savage Guns* (in original Spanish, *Tierra Brutal*) and is an example of how there's even less spaghetti in one of these films. Michael Carreras was an Englishman who had a background as a producer of British Hammer Horror movies. He had been the producer of the classic 1958 *Dracula* movie starring Christopher Lee. He had set up a new studio called Capricorn Productions with fellow Hammer alumnus Jimmy Sangster.

By 1960, Hollywood was producing fewer Westerns because they weren't as popular with American moviegoing audiences as they had been. The problem was that Europe couldn't get enough of them. So, Carreras spotted a gap in the market, and Britain rather incongruously got involved in the making of the Western. The market had changed immeasurably since 1899's *Kidnapping by Indians*, and nobody was going to buy Blackburn as the Wild West. So, Carreras decided to go to Spain, which at the time was still a dictatorship under General Franco, a man who had won the Spanish Civil War thanks to aid provided by Hitler. Because of this, Spain had not been much used in international film production, but the south of Spain, with its arid plateaus, could emulate a geographically vague part of the American frontier. In the end Almeria was chosen.

Carreras decided to get a B-list American actor to star, someone recognisable but without the price tag of a Gary Cooper or John Wayne, so that audiences both in America and beyond would see it as a legitimate Western. He chose Richard Basehart whose most famous role up to that point had been Ishmael in 1956's *Moby Dick*. There were a couple of Americans in other key roles, and the rest of the cast were local Spaniards whose lines were dubbed into English in post-production. And with this simple formula, the Spaghetti Western was born.

The plot of *The Savage Guns* was the standard fare of a civil war veteran who, seeking a new life and a fresh start, wanders into a town threatened by outlaws, and as a reluctant hero picks up his gun again to help the locals. The MPAA had issues with a scene showing the crushing of a hand (which was nothing for those used to British horror films), which started the Spaghetti Western's reputation for brutal, realistic violence. A B-list actor got a starring role, Spain got some revenue for location filming, Carreras got his first chance to direct, the Brits got an authentic-looking, low-cost movie, and the world got more Westerns. What's not to love when everyone wins?

Except the film didn't do very well internationally, which meant Carreras made a loss on his first film. Capricorn Productions was shut down, and Michael Carreras and Jimmy Sangster returned to Hammer where they went on to have successful careers. MGM distributed the film in America, and according to their own records, it made a nice profit. So, while Carreras's idea hadn't worked for him, he had created a way to make cheap Westerns, which done the right way, could make a tidy sum.

And that brings us to the first great Spaghetti Western, 1964's *A Fistful of Dollars* - or should that be *Per un Pugno di Dollari*, which, translated from the Italian would make it *For a Fistful of Dollars*. But then again, onscreen the film is called *Fistful of Dollars*, which brings us to the first problem with international movie making, translation. The accurate translation of any movie title is important, but to stop a paragraph like this appearing at the start of each new 'foreign' movie, I will henceforth refer to the film by its commonly accepted name.

As in the case of *The Savage Guns*, the Italian film director Sergio Leone chose as his hero an American actor known to US audiences but one who was certainly not a big star. Clint Eastwood had appeared in mediocre movies such as the World War I film *Hell Bent for Glory* and as Rowdy Yates in the very popular TV Western series *Rawhide*.

After more than 200 episodes of *Rawhide*, Eastwood didn't want to play another cowboy, and his contract with the show prohibited him from playing a cowboy in any American movies, the producers of the show never dreaming anyone would go to another country to film a Western. Eastwood was drawn to the script which he recognised as a Western interpretation of Akira Kurosawa's 1961 film *Yojimbo*.

In *Yojimbo*, a samurai (played by Toshiro Mifune) comes to town to discover two warring factions vying for control. The desperate villagers are caught between the two groups, and the higher authorities are powerless to intervene. Using his cunning, the samurai (called Sanjuro; hence the name of the sequel, *Yojimbo* means bodyguard, which is what he pretends to be in the film) plays one group off the other until they are suitably weakened to the point where he can finish them off in a tense, action-packed climax. While the clothing and culture of *Yojimbo* are very specific, the basic story can easily be repurposed into a Western, and so once again, Kurosawa influenced a classic American Western. The problem was that Leone hadn't bought the rights to *Yojimbo* and asked Eastwood to downplay the connection. They knew the Kurosawa influence, but the average cinemagoer would not.

Sergio Leone was still new to directing, having been credited on only one previous film, although it's widely believed he had an uncredited directorial role on another. Both films were cheap, uninspired sword-and-sandals' epics that Italy was cranking out at the time because again, Hollywood had stopped making them. With these in mind, the thinking was that Leone was just the man to do a cheap, uninspired Western. What nobody expected was the visionary piece of filmmaking that Leone would produce.

With long periods of no dialogue (which would be taken to a whole new level later in Eastwood's career) and many of the characters with several days growth of beard and a moral ambiguity conveyed by their clothing, the film was revolutionary. Thinking about it, of course men on the frontier would be dirty, sweaty and hairy, but that just hadn't been shown before. Wayne always appeared cleanly shaven or had a perfectly groomed moustache for a specific role. In Wayne's *The Alamo*, after more than a week of brutal siege warfare, when did the defenders have the time or even the motivation to shave? And yet, no one had even a five o'clock shadow. Another departure from the norm was that Leone used perspiration to show desperation in a way that was unique … and then there were the clothes. Tom Mix made it a virtual law that the good guy wore lighter-coloured clothing than the bad guy. Leone dressed everyone pretty much the same so that moral ambiguity was implied not just through their actions, but also in their appearance. Eastwood and Leone together created Eastwood's unique look: The actor brought a few parts of his Rawhide costume, but the poncho was bought in Spain and turned out to be the item that created his iconic look. Eastwood was a non-smoker and used his annoyance at having to smoke a cheroot to enhance his portrayal of his character. Leone summed up Eastwood's acting like this: "More than an actor, I needed a mask, and Eastwood, at that time, only had two expressions: with hat and no hat."

That might be harsh, but his acting style has also been described as dynamic lethargy. He can stand in frame for seconds doing nothing and make it interesting to watch; it also helps that he has a glare your unborn descendants can feel.

The film's shoot was relatively straightforward except it had an air of the Tower of Babel about it. The film was an Italian/German/Spanish co-production, so there was a significant language barrier on set. Leone could only speak Italian, so Eastwood communicated with him as well as the rest of the Italian cast and crew mainly through actor and stuntman Benito Stefanelli. Like other Italian films shot at the time, all the footage was filmed silent, and the dialogue and sound effects were dubbed in post-production.

The Hays Code specified that there needed to be a cut between someone firing a gun and someone being hit by the bullet. In *A Fistful of Dollars*, the first act of violence occurs in the marvellous scene where Eastwood asks some outlaws to apologise to his mule. In the resulting showdown, Eastwood is seen firing away in the foreground, and the men go down in the background. Hardly graphic violence by today's standards but shockingly brutal to American audiences of the time.

Then there's the music. Ennio Morricone was another Italian, who by the age of nineteen was writing music for theatre. By twenty-five he was writing for radio, and in the 50s he was writing and recording popular jazz compositions. Also, in the late 50s and early 60s he began composing scores for movies, including a few lesser Westerns. His composition for *A Fistful of Dollars* was unlike any Western score that came before it. Its opening, using a human whistler and tin whistles, was odd enough, but at least they were instruments used in the Old West. But when the electric guitar kicks in, we are catapulted into a completely anachronistic arrangement that works. The theme is that unique blend of something totally fresh and exciting and yet sounds like a classic composition.

A Fistful of Dollars didn't start the careers of any of the major players, but it took all of them to a whole new level. Eastwood broke out of TV, Leone became internationally recognised, and Morricone would go on to compose some of the most recognisable and beautiful film scores in history (when it comes to the signature tune from *The Mission*, I'm not crying, you're crying).

The whole production was made for less than a quarter of a million dollars and grossed the equivalent of over $4 million in Italy, making it at the time the biggest grossing movie in Italian film history. This, despite many scathing Italian reviews. It went on to be as big a hit in the rest of Europe, but it took years for it be released in America for fear of legal action from Kurosawa. In the end that didn't happen, but the film wasn't released in North America until 1967, where again, it made a heap of money, bringing the global box office total to nearly $20 million. Not only was it a smash hit, but unlike some of the big budget movies, it also turned an impressive profit.

If there's one thing the global movie industry loves, it's low-hanging fruit. The appeal of a sequel or a series of movies based on a major hit is that an audience is baked in, and the returns are guaranteed. It can be a law of diminishing returns but not always; if it worked once, let's do it again. In the case of the *Dollar* films, the titles could be said to have a double meaning: they tie into the first film's title for brand recognition, but they also play on their ability to make money. And so, *For a Few Dollars More* was born.

Eventually there would be three films known as the Dollars Trilogy or The Man with No Name Trilogy. Neither is particularly appropriate as the films are more closely linked by themes and style than actual story. Indeed, if *The Good, the Bad and the Ugly* is a prequel, how can Lee Van Cleef die in that and be walking around in *For a Few Dollars More*, albeit with a different name. Then there's Eastwood's character, called Joe in the first film, Manco in the second and Blondie in the third.

Despite the threat of legal wranglings over *Yojimbo* with the first film, the remaking of *Sanjuro* (the sequel to *Yojimbo*) would have been a logical choice for the sequel to *A Fistful of Dollars*, but Leone wanted nothing more to do with accusations of plagiarism, so 1965's *For a Few Dollars More* is its own thing. Once again Almeria in Spain was used for location shooting, and the interiors were done at Rome's Cinecittà Studios. Bigger, bolder, bloodier and more explosive, with an even weirder yet perfect theme tune, the gang was back to shock censors and thrill audiences. And, just to be clear, none of these films is even remotely going for historical authenticity; they are merely leaning into the myths of the Old West. The geography is wrong, the costumes are all over the place in terms of timeline, and the guns are more accurate than modern firearms, rather than the smooth-bore pistols of the era. But none of this matters. This is entertainment, pure and simple; the films are audio-visual experiences that rip the viewer from his humdrum life and drops them right in the middle of the visceral action. This is what cinema is meant to do, and John Wayne's noble cowboy wouldn't last five minutes in this bleak, morally ambiguous, sun-bleached landscape.

For a Few Dollars More got better reviews than its predecessor, and while it cost nearly three times as much to make, that still only came to $600,000. The film grossed over $25 million worldwide, making the

An image of a cowboy from the 1880s. This kind of iconic image would inspire movies for over a century. (*Wikimedia*)

Lobby card for the remake of the Three Godfathers. A film so influential it would end up being made three times. (*moviestillsdb*)

Buster Keaton created his magnum opus with the highly ambitious, and expensive, The General which has about every stunt you can conduct on a train. (*moviestillsdb*)

Tom Mix, the iconic silent era cowboy who innovated the genre by building a frontier town to film many of his films on the same location. (*Wikimedia*)

All the promotional material implied an epic action movie, instead it was an epic drama which would go on to win the Best Picture Academy Award, the first western to do so. (*moviestillsdb*)

In such a macho world as the wild west, Annie Oakley as a woman who was good with a gun fascinated during her lifetime and later in cinema. (*moviestillsdb*)

The Call of the Wild is an example of a western that breaks most of the rules, its snow not desert and the Klondike is in Canada and Alaska. (*moviestillsdb*)

While Stagecoach was far from John Wayne's first film, it was the one that launched him to stardom. Despite being The Ringo Kid he was already in his 30s. (*moviestillsdb*)

Ian McShane plays Al Swearengen, and boy did he and all the other cast swear in HBO's highly acclaimed Deadwood. (*moviestillsdb*)

Tarantino revitalises the western for a new millennium with Django Unchained. It's his most financially successful film he directed to date. (*moviestillsdb*)

Promotional image for the TV series Gunsmoke, it ran for literally decades but was abruptly cancelled. (*moviestillsdb*)

David Oyelowo plays Bass Reeves in the prestige Paramount+ series. Reeves was a real lawman and has garnered more deserved attention over the last 15 years. (*moviestillsdb*)

Westworld would be relaunched as a prestige drama on HBO in 2016. (*moviestillsdb*)

One of the most successful westerns of all time was the comedy Blazing Saddles. Critics thought it was crude, audiences thought it was hilarious. (*moviestillsdb*)

Is Last of the Mohicans a western? It's in America, with lots of Native Americans, but it's all muskets and redcoats rather than cowboys and revolvers. Either way it's a great film. (*moviestillsdb*)

Promotional image of Clint Eastwood's Unforgiven, quite rightly another 90s western drowning in box office and Academy Awards. (*moviestillsdb*)

Yul Brynner plays a robot cowboy in Westworld a possible precursor to the terminator. (*moviestillsdb*)

Cimino made a magnificent movie with Heaven's Gate, unfortunately his spending and hubris were out of control. The film is too long, too languid and his profligate spending bankrupted a movie studio. (*moviestillsdb*)

Kevin Costner brought Oscar gold and massive box office back to the western in 1990. It led to a slew of high profile westerns in the 90s. (*moviestillsdb*)

1966's Django took the already brutal reputation of the Spaghetti Western and turned it up to boiling point failing to get an official rating classification in Britain for decades. (*moviestillsdb*)

While Butch Cassidy and the Sundance Kid is considered a classic western, it's set after 1900 and much of the action takes places in South America. (*moviestillsdb*)

Eastwood and Leone explode onto the screen with one of the greatest Spaghetti Westerns based, unofficially, on one of the greatest Japanese movies of all time. (*moviestillsdb*)

The Good, the Bad and the Ugly is not only one of the greatest westerns of all time, but many consider it one of the greatest films of all time, with the highest score of any film on Rotten Tomatoes without being nominated for a single Oscar. (*moviestillsdb*)

While Paint Your Wagon was a successful musical at the time, today it is an oddity and proof why neither Marvin nor Eastwood pursued a singing career. (*moviestillsdb*)

Who wore it better? Jeff Bridges (2010) and John Wayne (1969) in costume as Rooster Cogburn. (*moviestillsdb*)

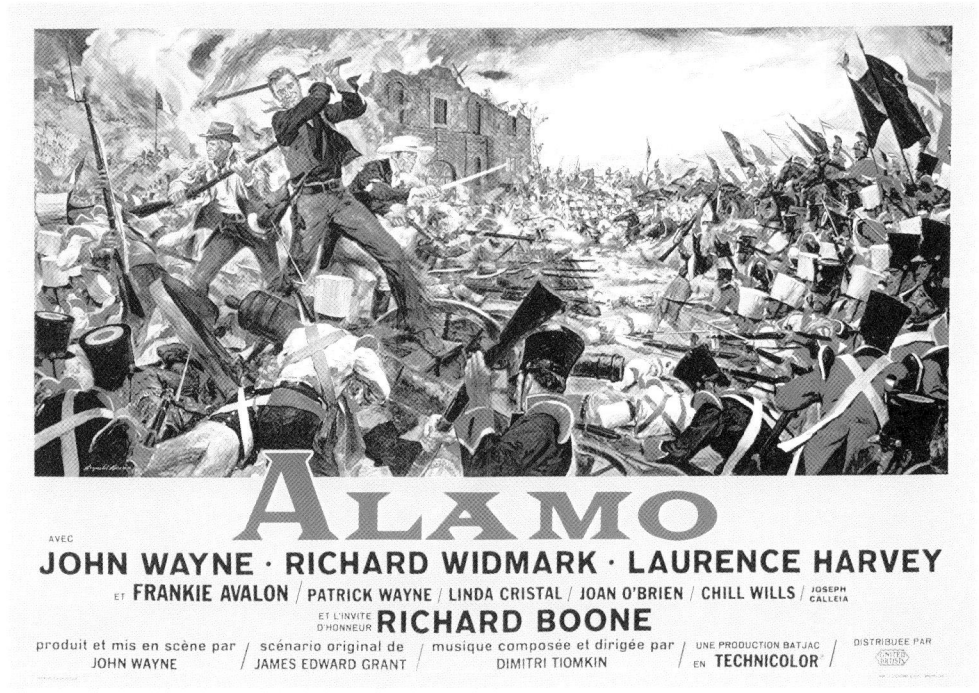

While the Alamo was a huge hit, it was also ruinously expensive for star and director John Wayne. It didn't help that it was not well reviewed. In 2004 Disney tried again with even worse financial results. (*moviestillsdb*)

Yul Brynner was meant to be the star, but in this still from the Magnificent Seven you can see how Steve McQueen by choosing a different pose grabs attention. (*moviestillsdb*)

Iconic image from the end of the Searchers, the slightly awkward pose was Wayne showing respect to Harry Carey who was a friend and Carey's widow and son were in the film. (*moviestillsdb*)

Oklahoma! As a smash hit this musical shows the diversity of the genre. From crime thriller, to historical drama to action movie, westerns can even be musicals. (*moviestillsdb*)

Olivia de Havilland and Errol Flynn in Dodge City would recreate the chemistry and box office of their previous partnerships. Note the mirrored pose of protection between this image and the one from High Noon. (*moviestillsdb*)

Publicity still for Shane, gritty for its time with one of the most iconic endings in cinema history. (*moviestillsdb*)

Does Doris Day play a lesbian in this film? It wasn't shot that way at the time, but today it sure seems that way. (*moviestillsdb*)

The Colt Single Action Army Revolver. Although the historical western frontier had many firearms used, this was the definitive revolver that appeared in literally hundreds of westerns. (*Wikimedia*)

Grace Kelly and Gary Cooper in a publicity shot for High Noon, one of the greatest westerns ever made, which John Wayne thought was "un-American". (*moviestillsdb*)

whole project ludicrously profitable for all involved. Leone had wanted to get Henry Fonda and Charles Bronson in key roles, and although he couldn't get them interested at this point, he kept trying, and his approaches would eventually pay off.

Third time's a charm, right? The budget was once again doubled. Clint Eastwood could now demand a quarter of a million dollars and a Ferrari as his fee, a big step up from his $15,000 for *A Fistful of Dollars*. The reality was that even if the movie brought in half the revenue of the first one, it would still be hugely profitable and so filming began on the extremely ambitious *The Good, the Bad and the Ugly*. Lee Van Cleef came back and Eli Wallach was added to the mix as Tuco. Eastwood was the good, Van Cleef was the bad, and poor old Wallach was the ugly. While Eastwood is the good, he kills more people than the other two leads combined. In reality, the film is Wallach's movie; he gets more screen time than anyone else, and his performance is so sensational he almost steals the greatest film of the trilogy away from Eastwood, the nominal star.

While the desolate villages clinging onto the barren landscape are still there, now we have full-blown battle scenes with hundreds of extras. The story, however, is similarly bleak: Eastwood and Wallach find out that there's buried gold worth $200,000; the problem is one of them knows which cemetery it's buried in, and the other knows which grave to dig. So, they need each other. Meanwhile, Van Cleef hears about the gold and is trying to hunt them down. The backdrop of this one is the US Civil War, and there is an epic battle for a bridge, which once again muddies the waters of the definition of the Western genre. Is this a war film or a Western? The pivotal bridge scene nearly didn't make it into the film. When it came time to blow up the bridge, Leone instructed the Spanish army captain in charge to trigger the fuse. He was involved because the Spanish army had helped build the bridge and supplied a lot of the extras. The two of them had previously agreed to blow up the bridge when Leone gave the signal "Vai!" (Go!) over the walkie-talkie. Unfortunately, another crew member spoke on the same channel, saying the words, "Vai, vai!", meaning, "It's okay, proceed" to a second crew member. The captain heard this signal and blew up the bridge. Unfortunately, no cameras were running at the time. Leone was so upset he fired the crewman, who promptly fled from the set. The captain was so sorry for what happened that he proposed to Leone that the Army would rebuild the bridge to blow it up again, with one condition: that the fired crewman be re-hired. Leone agreed, the crewman was forgiven, the bridge was rebuilt, and the scene was, finally, successfully shot.

Eastwood was, as it turned out, a little too close to the bridge the second time. When it blows, real rubble can be seen raining down all over the area, and one rock falls just inches from Eastwood's head. Had it struck him it almost certainly would have killed him. Health and safety were not high priorities on any of these films. Wallach was told to lie near the train tracks and allow the train to roll over and break his chains, but as the train approached, Leone realised that while there was plenty of clearance between Eli's head and the locomotive, that wasn't the case at the end of the carriages, each of which had a metal step down. By now the train was too close to Wallach for him to hear the warning, but had he lifted his head just a little he would have been decapitated.

This was still the grey period for the safety of horses. The American Humane Association began its work in film in 1940 after an incident that occurred on the set of the film *Jesse James*. The group began protesting the public release of the film because of a scene in which a horse was forced to run off the edge of a cliff. The horse fell over 70 feet to the ground below, broke its spine and had to be put down. A standard way in old Westerns for a horse to go down pretending it had either been shot or bitten by a snake was to pull out one of the horse's legs with a wire. This would at the very least cause bruising, and in some cases, led to a broken leg, meaning the horse would have to be put down. Such acts are now banned. In 1980, the release of *Heaven's Gate* was met with national picketing and protests after complaints about how the filming had involved the inhumane treatment of animals – including the deaths of five horses. The Screen Actors Guild negotiated for the universal presence of a member of the American Humane Association (AHA) on the set as part of its union deal, forcing moviemakers to contact AHA in advance of any animal being present on set. Today, AHA is best known for its certification mark that "No Animals Were Harmed", which appears at the end of film or television credits where animals are featured. If the stars of *The Good, the Bad and the Ugly* were put in danger, it is unlikely that any kind of animal care was given, but if there were any specific incidents, they were not recorded.

The onscreen cruelty was just as shocking. Seeing the handsome Eastwood covered in blisters from extreme sunburn may have been achieved with chewing gum, but he looks hideously disfigured. With the beatings in the prisoner-of-war camp and the slapping of a defenceless woman (which Van Cleef refused to do, and a stunt man was used as a body double), this is a brutal and nihilistic film.

After his two previous amazing soundtracks, Ennio Morricone outdid himself again. Is there anyone who has not heard those eight notes that introduce the theme? The theme becomes a motif throughout the film, and the motif becomes a slice of audio perfection. The cinematography as well is sensational. The three men positioned in the ultimate standoff at the end is one of the tensest pieces of cinema ever made and made doubly so when it's just three men standing there, doing nothing but staring at each other for over four minutes. That score and the cameras focused on those intense, sweaty stares are more exciting than a dozen *Fast and Furious* films put together. At the time the critics hated it, particularly the American critics, who looked down on the cheap, foreign subgenre that was the Spaghetti Western, a term that was never meant as a compliment. Over the years however, the film was re-evaluated by a new generation brought up on Eastwood, not Wayne. Today *The Good, the Bad and the Ugly* is regarded as a classic, up there with *The Godfather* and *Citizen Kane,* and is the highest-rated movie on IMDb, Metacritic and Rotten Tomatoes never to have been nominated for an Oscar. IMDb even has it at number 10 in its top 250 movies of all time.

But this was not a case of a cult hit slowly making its money back after being shown in late-night movie slots and later video rentals. This trilogy of films is that rare example of each one getting better reviews and each one in turn making more money. This film's initial costs were around $1.2 million, and the worldwide gross was nearly $39 million.

But this was not the only Spaghetti Western success of 1966. If Sergio Leone could crank them out quick and cheap, then Sergio Corbucci could make them quicker and cheaper ... but probably not as good. He had two notable Spaghetti Westerns out in the same year (of a total of four, showing the appetite in the market for the films, rather than any concern for their quality): *Django* and *Navajo Joe*. *Django* bravely broke one of the rules of making these European Westerns by casting the full-blooded, proud Italian Franco Nero, rather than a B-list American. But the movie was still filmed in Almeira, Spain, still recorded silent with audio added later, and still paid g no attention to the MPAA Hays Code in America. It opens with a woman being mercilessly whipped by a bunch of bandits, and the violence and sadism doesn't stop there. It's basically *Yojimbo* again, only with the brilliantly novel twist that the titular hero is wearing a Union uniform and dragging a coffin. For a large part of the movie the viewer only wants to know why he has the coffin and what's in it. The film was a leap forward in brutality in the same way *A Fistful of Dollars* was a leap forward in graphic violence from a more conventional Western like *Rio Bravo*. There's a scene where an ear is cut off and the victim is forced to eat it, which the Italian censors asked to be removed to achieve certification, but the editor "forgot" to cut it.

The ghost town in *The Good, the Bad and the Ugly* had originally been the set built for *Django* which was filmed on a micro budget. As Nero was only twenty-three, he was cheap but oh, so handsome! The film is a classic exploitation or grindhouse film with just enough violence, plot and pretty girls to keep an undemanding audience happy, but it was inferior in every way to Leone's Spaghetti Westerns. Nevertheless, it did big business in Italy, but with its scenes of graphic violence, it took decades for *Django* to get a rating in Britain (it finally passed in 1993) and wasn't given official distribution in America until 1972. Because of its notoriety and the difficulty in trying to copywrite a proper name (and the film had already ripped off an existing property), there were more than thirty unofficial sequels. There was one official sequel called *Django Strikes Again*, starring Nero, released in 1987. It was, of course, completely rebooted by Quentin Tarantino with 2012's *Django Unchained*, which will be explored later and did have a cameo with Nero in it.

Corbucci's other notable film of 1966 was *Navajo Joe*. This is the story of an outlaw gang massacring a tribe of peaceful Navajos. The sole survivor, Joe, plots his revenge and pursues the outlaws on their way to the small town of Esperanza. This is quite a pleasing plot to the modern viewer. Highlighting the cruelty that white settlers inflicted on the indigenous population is the topic that won Oscars for *Dances with Wolves*. It's all good until you find out that while Corbucci did get the American actor Burt Reynolds, he was not the right ethnicity to play the titular Navajo Joe. While the topic is progressive, the tone absolutely is not. The modern term for Burt Reynolds dressed up in native garb is cultural appropriation, but that is overthinking the basic revenge plot that Corbucci was going for. The film is a rare instance where the Native American is the good guy, and the white cowboys are the bad guys. It's just a shame they picked Reynolds for the lead role.

Allegedly, Burt Reynolds only agreed to make this film because he was under the impression that Sergio Leone would be directing. He was a fan of the Dollar movies and saw what they had done for Clint Eastwood's career. When he found out it was Sergio Corbucci, he tried to pull out, but the contracts had already been signed, and it was too late. While Reynolds is miscast, he gives a good performance in what is a B-movie. Reynolds did have a sense of humour about the whole affair, saying the movie is "so awful, it was shown only in prisons and airplanes because nobody could leave".

Reynolds had one consolation: Ennio Morricone composed the score. Never heard it? There's a reason for that. Presumably he scribbled it on the back of a cigarette packet while he was putting all his effort into

The Good, the Bad and the Ugly because, in the author's opinion, it's his worst work. Don't believe me? Watch the trailer on YouTube, and if you disagree, I'm @jemduducu on X (formally Twitter) and Threads.

If Sergio Corbucci could do two films in a year, Lee Van Cleef could do more, and in 1967, he starred in three Spaghetti Westerns. All were shot in Spain, all were incredibly cheap to produce and all were profitable for Van Cleef. In each one he played the older, wiser mentor, fixing problems, sometimes by tough talking but usually by filling people with holes.

The first of Van Cleef's films, *The Big Gundown* was directed by Sergio Sollima and even got a Morricone score. It's pretty good but nothing groundbreaking. All these films are unsavoury, grimy in their stories and darker than Leone ever was. Van Cleef plays a retired bounty hunter who is forced to take one last job after a twelve-year-old girl is raped and killed. The assault is not onscreen, but couldn't killing her be motivation enough? We are now heading to the 1970s, and as a number of film critics have pointed out, the amount of rapes in 70s' cinema is deeply worrying. *The Big Gundown* simply takes Leone's formula and adds more violence, torture and blood.

The second of Van Cleef's trilogy is *Death Rides a Horse*, directed by Giulio Petroni. This is a great title for a Western, but again, we are in very dark territory. Fellow American John Phillip Law plays Bill, who was a boy when his father was killed and his mother and sister were gang raped and murdered in front of him by four outlaws. Fifteen years later he meets up with former outlaw Van Cleef to exact his revenge. It's a similar story to 1969's *True Grit*, but this is tonally completely different, and again, rape rears its ugly head.

Finally, there was *Day of Anger*, directed by Tonino Valerii. A street cleaner becomes the student of a famed gunfighter (that'll be Lee Van Cleef), and they work together to fight outlaws trying to take over the town. This film is the lightest of the three, and besides the full cut, it has a shorter one with the more shocking scenes of violence taken out.

In all three of these movies Lee Van Cleef takes on the role of the tutor who helps a younger man exact revenge or learn the skills to do so.

Think of him as a grumpier, more lethal version of Obi Wan Kenobi. The films meant three substantial pay days for Van Cleef who was riding high after *The Good, the Bad and the Ugly*. All of his films are solid Westerns; certainly there are worse films in this book, it's just that they lacked originality and don't stand out as important in the genre. They are mentioned here to show that once the Spaghetti Western formula had been perfected, Europe churned them out at an astonishing rate. And while Sergio Leone may have been the best in the business, he was not the only horse in the race. The quality of these European films varied wildly, and while the style was always different to the average American 50s' Western, the results were no better or worse just because they were coming from another continent.

After *The Good, the Bad and the Ugly*, Leone felt he had done everything he wanted to do in the genre and started working on an idea for a gangster movie that would eventually become *Once Upon a Time in America*. Meanwhile, Paramount was desperate for him to make another Western and basically gave him everything he had ever wanted to make it, including Henry Fonda, Charles Bronson and a colossal $5 million budget. How could he say no? Obviously, he said yes and went to work on a film that would eventually become 1968's *Once Upon a Time in the West*.

Fonda had to be convinced and initially turned down the role of the villain of the piece. Leone flew to America to meet Fonda who asked why he was wanted for the film. Leone replied, "Picture this: the camera shows a gunman from the waist down pulling his gun and shooting a running child. The camera pans up to the gunman's face and …it's Henry Fonda!" Fonda had made a career of playing the nice, reliable guy. This was a chance to play a completely different character, and after it was put like that, Fonda grabbed it with both hands. Turns out Fonda's portrayal made his character one of the coldest villains in cinema history.

Bronson was second choice to Eastwood who felt he had served his time with Leone and was off doing his own thing, which in 1968, was the Alistair Maclean penned action-adventure set in World War II called *Where Eagles Dare*. It is ironic that in all the very adult and very bloody films Eastwood has ever made, he killed more onscreen people in *Where Eagles Dare* (suitable for all audiences) than in any other movie.

In *Once Upon a Time in the West*, Woody Strode, mentioned in *The Man Who Shot Liberty Valance*, is one of three men waiting at the station. Originally, there was meant to be a score, but instead, it's just the squeaky sound of a swinging sign, water dripping on a hat, the buzzing of a fly. The first eight minutes are just gunmen waiting around. The acting and the direction are powerful but subtle. These men do not shout and wave their guns around; they are cool, under-pressure professionals ready for action. We know there's going to be trouble, but we don't know why or when. Once again, Leone plays with our expectations, and we are instantly drawn in.

Fonda had a love scene with a completely naked actress, a new experience for him ... and his wife, who was on set during the filming. Bronson was the hero who spends more time playing the harmonica than talking, hence his name Harmonica, and Morricone was on hand to write another eery score. This time the main theme was not that memorable, but Harmonica's theme, played and replayed in snatches throughout the film, is haunting and sinister, particularly when the guitar kicks in.

As usual, there's an ugly beauty in all Leone's shots, and the sweeping vistas, including the widest and most ambitious panning shot so far filmed, is exactly what Paramount wanted to lure TV viewers back into the theatres. Once again, all the men are sweaty and stubbly. Leone uses Fonda's piercing blue eyes to great effect as they are in juxtaposition to his dark outfit and tanned skin.

Leone had a big enough budget to film in the US (Monument Valley, of course), but about half of it went on salaries. The plot is simplicity itself: a gunslinger joins forces with a notorious outlaw to protect a beautiful widow from a ruthless villain working for the railroad. It's not Shakespeare, but Leone gives us one of the best directed films ever made. Is it better than *The Good, the Bad and the Ugly*? That's up to you, but it's certainly of the same quality. *Once Upon a Time in the West* was long and contained scenes that the MPAA were only just then getting to grips with (in devising a new system of ratings), so the Americans got a cutdown version (because they were thought to have shorter attention spans and were less accepting of graphic violence), and it took time to come out. The watered-down version got poor reviews, but the film did well at the box office. Initially, because of the issues with its distribution in North America, the film didn't make its money back, but over the years, and now with a fully restored cut, its reputation has only grown, and *Once Upon a Time in the West* finally went into profit.

In 1971, Sergio Leone returned for one last Western, *Duck you Sucker!* Or the longer version known as *A Fistful of Dynamite*. This was a high- concept story about an outlaw and an IRA explosives' expert helping out in the Mexican Revolution. It stars Rod Steiger and James Coburn, and it's a good film if you can get around the politics. Having a member of the IRA as a hero in a film released in the heart of the Troubles, when civilians on both sides were dying in bombings, was hard for many audiences to swallow. The tone is more rowdy adventure than his other Westerns, but the political background was then current and nothing to laugh about.

Meanwhile, Sergio Corbucci wasn't finished adding his own blend of bleak and hyperviolent films to the genre. We're about halfway through this book, and already almost every Western genre rule has been broken. Native Americans have been the good guys as well as the bad guys. We've had morality tales and films so violent they failed to achieve a rating for decades. There have been heroes so morally ambiguous the term "anti-hero" was coined for them, and yet, despite all these various deviations, one rule had remained intact: the bad guys always lose. Until we come to 1968's *The Great Silence*.

The Great Silence is a fascinating film because it goes out of its way to confound as many expectations as possible. Not filmed in the sun-baked plains of southern Spain, instead, we are in the Alps as Corbucci depicts the great blizzard of 1899. The highly respected French actor Jean-Louis

Trintignant plays Silence the hero, who is mute, which takes the near silent protagonist to its logical limits. This helps in at least one respect as otherwise this Frenchman would have had to be dubbed into English. And the great German actor Klaus Kinski (who appeared as a hunchback in *For a Few Dollars More*) plays the antagonist Loco. The film may be based on a real moment in American meteorological history, but that was it for accuracy. The outlaws are referred to in the translations and in all the material around the movie as "bounty killers", but that's not the correct term; they should be called "bounty hunters" - except they do not act like them either. The men are simply bandits, outlaws. I have no idea why they were given this specifically wrong label.

Due to the necessarily snowbound location, the production was more expensive than Corbucci's previous movies, and the studio scenes had to be dressed with all kinds of materials including shaving foam. The production itself was inspired by very recent political assassinations; those of Che Guevara and Malcolm X had especially saddened him, and in 1968, Bobby Kennedy and Martin Luther King were also killed by gunmen's bullets. If the times were politically bleak, why not reflect that in a film. The oppressive atmosphere of the movie perfectly portrays this as does the title as it seemed in the late 60s that many great reformers were being silenced.

Of course, to drastically confound the audience by not giving them what they want can have implications. Corbucci understood this and shot two endings, one had an ambiguous conclusion and the other had a more satisfactory, traditional end. In an unusually brave move, the producers decided to go with the ambiguous ending, the one that was more emotionally realistic and ends with the bad guys gunning down the protagonist.

Corbucci never had love scenes in his films, and the roles for women were always under-written. But in this film he continued with the social commentary. Vonetta McGee (an African American actress) plays Pauline, a woman who seduces Silence as she tends to his wounds. She had rebuffed the outlaws and chooses Silence, a move she hopes will serve as her revenge. She is the one in control, and the mixed-race love scene drove American censors crazy. In any other Western she would get what she wants, but in this bleak version of the Old West, she is gunned down along with the hero. It is an agonising moment in a movie full of melancholy and regret. The film did alright at the box office, but it was not a smash hit, however, as with this conceit and that ending it was never aiming for mass market appeal. The film was designed not to please everyone. The strong sense of injustice that the film elicits is exactly what Corbucci was going for.

Hollywood watched the Hays Code pass into history and decided to get bloody in its own way. 1969 saw the creation of two classics in this new kind of bleak and bloody Western. The first was a film, which while definitely a Western, was set in 1913, so we are now in the 20th century. The story concerns an ageing gang of outlaws who cannot adjust to the rapidly changing world around them. As such, the film is full of older actors, those who would have played supporting roles in the tamer Westerns of a decade earlier. Here was the kindly uncle hero, except now he was angry and out for bloody revenge. *The Wild Bunch* were played by William Holden, Ernest Borgnine, Robert Ryan, Edmond O'Brien, Ben Johnson and Warren Oates, all true-blue Americans who spoke English. No need for dubs and the incongruous lack of lip synching. The director was Sam Peckinpah, a man who had risen through the ranks of inauspicious TV and a few run-of-the mill movies. Nobody was expecting him to make this bolt of lightning which led to his reputation for directing exhilaratingly bloody films in many genres, including *Straw Dogs*, *The Getaway* and *Cross of Iron*.

The Wild Bunch tells the story of the gang going down to Mexico to take out a general who has taken control of a town and the surrounding farms. The plot is familiar, but the gun violence is exceptional. The opening robbery was edited in a way that had never been seen before and influenced action cinema for decades. All gunfire in the movies used the same stock sounds and so, regardless of calibre or the surrounding environment, all pistols sounded the same (the same firearm sounds very different depending on whether it is fired in the middle of a field or in an enclosed indoor space). The same thing was true of rifle fire, and again, the same stock sound effects were used for all cannons as well as machine guns. So frustrated was Peckinpah by the samey-ness of these effects that he took a loaded revolver and fired live rounds into the wall, shouting "THAT'S the effect I want!" The attention to the detail of the action changed Hollywood cinema forever. There is a throughline from Peckinpah to John Woo or John McTiernan or Chad Stahelski. The emphasis was now on violence, and as much effort went into the fight choreography as the script.

The Wild Bunch tells a story that had been hinted at in the past but was brought viscerally to life. Time marches on, we all have our part to play, but then we are gently pushed to the sidelines and eventually off stage. You can't stop progress, and the old ways aren't necessarily the best ways. The film is a meditation on the passing of youth and the feeling of slow redundancy as you get older, but these middle-aged men are going down in a last great hurrah. The final, wildly bloody shootout is mythmaking at its best. *The Wild Bunch* become the 300 Spartans at Thermopylae or the defenders at the Alamo. They may go down, but they go down swinging and take dozens of the enemy with them in a mixture of slow motion, kinetic editing and lots and lots of bullets and blood.

There was fun on the set. Robert Ryan wouldn't stop complaining about not receiving top billing, and Peckinpah decided to get his subtle revenge. In the opening credits, the faces of William Holden and Ernest Borgnine are frozen in onscreen closeups while their names are listed. Peckinpah froze closeups of several horses' rear ends as Ryan was listed. Then there's the scene where Ben Johnson and Warren Oates fool around in huge wine vats with some local Mexican women … except the women weren't actresses but sex workers from a nearby brothel, hired by Peckinpah so he could tell people that Warner Bros had paid for hookers for his cast.

All of this to one side, America had learned from Europe, and its retort was every bit as beautifully bloody. The reviews were universally glowing; some even conveyed a sense of relief that finally America was creating modern Westerns. It is worth remembering that *The Wild Bunch* and the next film, *Butch Cassidy and the Sundance Kid*, both came out in the same year as *True Grit* and *Paint Your Wagon*. The differences between the first two and the other two couldn't be more different. *The Wild Bunch*, with a more adult rating was not going to match *Paint Your Wagon* or *True Grit* at the box office, but it did well enough to make money.

The second film mentioned earlier as a classic of this new kind of Western was based on the story of Robert LeRoy Parker and Harry Alonzo Longabaugh, better known as Butch Cassidy and the Sundance Kid. This movie shows Butch Cassidy and his gang (who were originally called the Wild Bunch, which was changed at the last minute to the Hole in the Wall Gang because *The Wild Bunch*, had been released just a few months earlier, and nobody wanted to confuse the two gangs – or the two films) robbing trains and banks. To be fair, that's what he and the Sundance Kid actually did, but it's safe to say they didn't do it with the panache, wit and movie star good looks of Paul Newman and Robert Redford. However, unlike *The Wild Bunch*, this film portrays real people, so let's have a look at what's onscreen versus what actually happened.

The gang formed in 1896, and the crimes they committed came at the very end of what could be considered the Wild West. Cassidy and his gang were cold-blooded murderers, not cheeky scamps on fun adventures. One of the gang members shot and killed a sheriff; they were dangerous men. The film isn't far off the truth, but the tone is distinctly biased. We are meant to love these guys even though you wouldn't ever want to meet them in real life. Butch Cassidy's younger sister Lula Parker Betenson was on the set during filming and would tell the cast and crew stories about her brother. Yet another reason to show these outlaws as relatable characters.

Tonally and utterly different, *The Wild Bunch* and *Butch Cassidy and the Sundance Kid* are about the same thing: the end of an era. By the start of the 20th century, society and technology had caught up with the old ways. There was nowhere left to hide, and these men, who only knew one thing, were doomed by the unstoppable march of progress. The films have similar endings but are shot in very different ways.

In the first half of *Butch Cassidy and the Sundance Kid*, the men are trying to escape a group of Pinkerton agents. Pinkerton was a genuine organisation (which still exists today), and in the 19th century, was the largest private law enforcement organisation in the world. Their agents would do dubious things like infiltrate trade unions to disrupt them from within, but they also undertook regular law enforcement work (as shown in the film), where they acted like a cross between US Marshals and bounty hunters. It was the gang's own fault that they were being pursued. In 1899, they had agreed an amnesty with the Governor of Utah: all they had to do was stop robbing trains. But they couldn't help themselves, and by the summer of 1900, they were at it again. In December of that year the gang posed for a photo which gave law enforcement an up-to-date picture of its five members; these guys were much dumber than the film portrays.

It's true that Cassidy and Sundance managed to escape and wound up in South America. Etta Place, Butch's partner, was a real woman, portrayed in the film as a teacher, but she was, in fact, a sex worker. They set up in Argentina and by 1905, there were reports of two English speaking robbers operating in the country. By 1908, the two men plus Etta had moved hundreds of miles north into Bolivia, where they robbed the payroll intended for a silver mine. This got the attention of the local authorities. What happens next is the stuff of legend, and the final scene in the film is a freeze frame with the sound of volley fire over it. If you've seen the film, you know it takes dozens of Bolivian soldiers to bring down our two brave anti-heroes. In reality, there were just three armed soldiers at the shootout. You read that right, three men, not thirty. It seems that once the gunfire stopped, soldiers entered the hut to find that Sundance had been mortally wounded and Butch had shot him to put him out of his misery, then shot himself.

The end of this film reflects the end of the Wild West. The stark contrast between the reality and the legends perpetuated by Hollywood come together in this one poignant moment from history. The ending is like that of *The Wild Bunch* but done in a very different way. Peckinpah influenced action cinema, but the director of *Butch Cassidy and the Sundance Kid*, George Roy Hill, created the first buddy movie where two mismatched people slowly come together to take on the real enemy. This new buddy dynamic inspired the likes of *Starsky and Hutch* and *Lethal Weapon*.

Despite what looks like harmony onscreen, the film set wasn't like that. In reality, George Roy Hill clashed with almost everyone. Katharine Ross (who played Etta) said simply, "Any day away from George Roy Hill was a good one". There is a great moment in the film when the gang is being chased by a relentless group of Pinkerton agents. At one point they leap on horseback almost supernaturally from a steam train carriage. In order to get the shot, the door on the opposite side of the train was left open and a ramp placed out of view. The riders then simply rode through the carriage to make the leap. In real life, the horses would not have had room in the carriage to make such a dramatic exit.

Butch Cassidy and the Sundance Kid even had a musical interlude courtesy of Burt Bacharach's "Raindrops Keep Falling on my Head" which would go on to win an Oscar; the film won four in total. On the one hand it's a delightful romp which older audience members could get behind, but on the other hand, we are following the outlaws and not the law. The men are anti-heroes, they are breaking the law and deserve to be brought to justice, and they are … off screen … to the grim sound of rifle volley fire.

The reviews at the time were average to low. People saw it as a slick, sanitised version of real events which lacked the bite of something like *The Wild Bunch* or even the Dollars Trilogy. That said, audiences didn't just like it, they loved it. This is the first film in this book (chronologically) where a global gross of over $100 million can be mentioned. With the same budget as *The Wild Bunch*, it grossed more than *The Wild Bunch*,

Paint Your Wagon and *True Grit* combined. It was the number one movie in the world for that year. Who cared if the critics were lukewarm about it.

The film was to accidentally herald a very modern trend in movie making. It was such a colossal hit that there was an appetite for more, but how could you do that when the heroes die at the end of the film? The answer, make a prequel.

In 1979 *Butch and Sundance: The Early Years* came out. Neither of the original stars returned and it was a huge flop. It also came out the same year as *Zulu Dawn* which was technically a prequel to the movie *Zulu*. But as these were historical events, the latter was often described as "the events leading up to *Zulu*". In the case of Butch and Sundance, the word "prequel" was actually used. Today, entire film franchises count on the concept of the prequel and yet it was the western that started the trend. Of course, one of the most famous westerns of all was a prequel- *The Good, the Bad and The Ugly*, but that term was never used at the time. This genre then paved the way for all those blockbuster sequels now filling the multiplex.

Robert Altman became a red-hot director after the smash hit *MASH*, the 1970 film about a field hospital in the Korean War. It was a highly subversive take on war films, and Altman was hoping to pull off something similar in the Western genre with 1971's *McCabe & Mrs Miller*. Altman described the film as an anti-Western made to deliberately subvert many of the tropes and moral themes of the genre. While this might have been his intention, he didn't get the plaudits he was after as many of these tropes had already been demolished in the Spaghetti Westerns.

The film was based on a 1959 novel by Edmund Naughton called simply McCabe. But as the film title suggests, a more egalitarian approach was taken with the characters, and so we have Warren Beatty playing McCabe and Julie Christie playing Mrs Miller. The film has moments that feel inspired by Beatty's role as Clyde Barrow in 1967's *Bonnie and Clyde*. The plot revolves around a gambler and a sex worker who become business partners and set up a brothel in a mining town. Their enterprise thrives until a large corporation arrives on the scene. In both cases Beatty plays a loveable anti-hero ultimately crushed by "the man" (to put it into 60's parlance). Of course, Clyde Barrow was a real gangster and that's a whole other story, but we get to see Beatty looking gorgeous in a suit while being morally flexible. The titular business partners become romantically entangled, but as a running joke, she still charges for her services. Like *The Great Silence* and *Call of the Wild* this isn't set in a sun-drenched arid plain, but in snowy mountains, where the locals are shivering not sweating.

The climactic shootout ends with Mrs Miller incapacitated in an opium den, and McCabe, wounded while killing his nemesis, bleeding out in the snow, ignored by the townsfolk who are busy putting out a fire. The anti-hero dies with a whimper rather than in a cacophonous climax. It's clever, but if you've seen *The Great Silence,* it's not new (although Altman is undoubtedly the better director with more resources).

Filming took place in Vancouver (cheaper than the US), a location that turned out to be full of young Americans dodging the Vietnam draft and readily available to work as extras. Snowfall nearly ruined the final climactic shoot, but the snow was incorporated into the downbeat ending. Reviews were mixed: some critics loved the new angle on a very old genre and admired the focus on a sexually empowered woman (a rarity in Westerns); others thought it was little too pleased with itself and that those tropes were there for a reason. In the end the film did well rather than blowing the doors off the box office. It remains a well-respected work if not the first film that comes to mind when thinking about more mature Westerns.

As we head towards the end of the chapter, let's return to Clint Eastwood in the 70s. By now Eastwood had cut his teeth as a director with the twisted erotic thriller *Play Misty for Me* in 1971. By 1973, having played a DJ, a hard-nosed cop and having, of course, tried singing, he was ready to do another Western, but one that he would direct, 1973's *High Plains Drifter.*

The plot is familiar and straightforward: after the local marshal is killed, a stranger comes to town and is hired to organise the townsfolk to bring justice to the rampaging outlaws. Its part *High Noon*, part *A Fistful of Dollars*. This isn't a Spaghetti Western as it's directed by an American, stars an American and was filmed in America, but there is still a distinct whiff of Bolognese sauce about it. Eastwood takes Leone's signature style and makes it his own. He recognises the influence of the teacher but isn't slavishly copying him.

Eastwood went all-in on realism, which Leone never did. He had a small town built for real, which allowed shooting of the interiors on location for an added sense of realism. No back projection or painted backdrops here. The character of Marshal Duncan was played by Buddy Van Horn who had been Eastwood's stunt double a number of times before. This implies that Eastwood could be Duncan back from the grave, an interesting supernatural edge to the usual Western affair (Eastwood would explore this further in *Pale Rider*). But it's not all po-faced, and just as in Leone's movies there are times of dark humour.

It is worth pausing here to consider the situation and how it might have played out. A movie star, who has only directed once before, is given millions of dollars to make a film the way he wants, with no supervision. Because he is the star, the film could have been a self-indulgent mess, an incoherent, self-aggrandising box office dud. But it wasn't. *High Plains Drifter* cemented Eastwood's reputation as a talented director as well as an actor. Anyone can get lucky once, but it takes talent to be consistently lucky. The film not only got great reviews, it also did well at the box office - for a film with an adult rating.

As this chapter began with the fall of the Hays Code and the rise of the rating system, it's time to look at further developments. The advantage of the Hays Code was that everyone could go see any film. Now the studios were having to adjust to ratings. They might have made a great film, but if it had an R or X rating, not everyone could see it, great reviews notwithstanding. This meant that if a project was aimed at an adult market, it would probably get a smaller budget, which meant a lower risk and a lower threshold to turn a profit. Today, if a big studio movie goes a little too far with its family friendly blockbuster, the simplest solution is to take the scene out. Sometimes the more adult films, which studios assume will be niche, end up doing big business which, because the initial outlay was low, means they end up being far more profitable than some family films. 2016's *Deadpool* and 2019's *Joker* are two highly profitable examples.

Moving to 1976, Eastwood again directed himself in *The Outlaw Josey Wales*. The story is an amalgam of a few previously mentioned storylines. Josey Wales, a Missouri farmer, is driven to revenge for the murder of his wife and son by a band of pro-Union militants during the civil war. Wales joins a Confederate guerrilla band and makes a name for himself as a feared gunfighter. After the war, all the fighters, except for him, in Wales' group surrender to Union soldiers, but the Confederates end up being massacred. Wales becomes an outlaw and is pursued by both bounty hunters and Union soldiers.

While books had been a standard starting point in the previous chapter, in this chapter the idea of a Western based on a book has been virtually absent, particularly in Spaghetti Westerns, which didn't have the budgets to buy rights. This movie is based on author Asa Earl "Forrest" Carter's 1972 novel The Rebel Outlaw: Josey Wales (republished as Gone to Texas). Eastwood got the very best talent involved and reached out to the red-hot duo of Michael Cimino and Philip Kaufman to help with the script. Another notable behind-the-scenes meeting occurred when Eastwood met Sondra Locke with whom he would go on to have a fifteen-year relationship, during which time they appeared together in multiple movies.

The Outlaw Josey Wales is an anti-authoritarian film, and the message is clear: the government is sometimes the bad guy, and you have the right to protect yourself from it. Interestingly, this played well to both the left-wing libertarians of the counterculture and the paranoid right-wing militia/conspiracy theorists. In this regard the film has aged well, and the politics seem as relevant in the 21st century.

Again, like *High Plains Drifter* it was all filmed in America, but unlike *High Plains Drifter*, it wasn't originally Eastwood's film to direct. Phil Kaufman was first choice as director, but his clashes with Eastwood got angrier and more bitter until things came to a head one evening when Kaufman insisted on finding a beer can to use as a prop in the scene they were filming. While he was off looking, Eastwood ordered the cameraman to quickly shoot the scene before the light faded and then drove away, leaving before Kaufman returned. The next day Eastwood fired Kaufman. The sacking caused outrage amongst the Directors Guild of America and other important Hollywood executives. Because Kaufman had already completed the pre-production, pressure mounted on Warner Bros and Eastwood to back down, and their refusal to do so resulted in a fine, reported to be around $60,000. This resulted in the Director's Guild passing the Eastwood Rule which prohibits an actor or producer from firing the director and then personally taking on the director's role. So, a Western (well, a grumpy Clint Eastwood) rewrote contractual filmmaking.

While most of these films are worth a look, do not watch them back-to-back. There are only so many casual deaths the average human can deal with in a short amount of time. What these films show is that sixty or seventy years after the Western genre was created there were still fresh ways to tell these stories. Sometimes it was a story that subverted expectations, at other times it was the visual language that was taken into new and interesting areas. However, it was time once again for the Western to evolve. It was time to stop making them quick, cheap, vulgar and violent. It was time to make them classy.

Chapter 5

Oscar Bait

While it took some Westerns years to be recognised for the art they are, others were machine tooled from the boots up to exist for awards' consideration. To be clear, this does not mean they will win them. The Oscars are notorious for not picking up on the industry trends. *The Shawshank Redemption,* one of the best reviewed Hollywood movies of all time was nominated for a slew of Oscars but walked away empty-handed. Stanley Kubrick never won a Best Director Oscar. People in the industry and elsewhere wonder if they are relevant anymore. But here's the thing, the Oscars are THE awards to win. Other industries use phrases like "these are the Oscars of the _____ (fill in the blank) industry". Winning a major Oscar category still adds millions to the box office and home rentals. They may not be as important as they used to be. but there is still nothing else quite like them. So it is tempting for some studios to make a movie that is meant to win an Oscar, and the whole film then has so much love poured into it that the expectation is that it will take home something if not that Best Picture golden statue. Some projects are clearly more cynically engineered than others. One of the earliest uses of the term "Oscar bait" was in reference to *Fort Apache,* but the first time it was used, literally, as a marketing strategy was 1978's *The Deer Hunter.* The film's initial screening feedback was so terrible the film was shown in just one arthouse cinema with only an intellectual audience and members of the academy seeing it. It was only put out for general release once it had been nominated for nine Oscars, which got it some great reviews and made it a box office hit. When it won five golden statues, it was mission accomplished, everyone happy.

One of the key differences between an Oscar contender and a run-of-the-mill movie is effort. Corbucci made some highly entertaining Westerns, but they were cranked out quick and fast. While making any movie takes effort, as you will see in this chapter some efforts to bring the vision to the screen were truly herculean. Great effort was put into finding the right locations and researching relevant cultures and linguistics. This was not the case for, say, Spaghetti Westerns. Almeria worked, so go there, shoot the script, don't go over the budget, and even if the film is only modestly successful, everyone walks away with a fistful of lira. The intent and purpose of most filmmakers were different. The likes of Hawks and Ford wanted not only to entertain but to create something of merit too.

One of the ways to be considered a "worthy" Western is to have a sympathetic portrayal of native peoples and their culture. Of course, this leads us into the thorny issues around cultural appropriation and the white saviour. So, let's look at these issues in one go rather than repeating the same points each time.

The Encyclopaedia Britannica defines cultural appropriation as something that "takes place when members of a majority group adopt cultural elements of a minority group in an exploitative, disrespectful, or stereotypical way". This is a beautifully nuanced description it would be hard to argue with; however, harsher interpretations of the term (mostly online) often result in threats to anyone believed to be guilty. So, it's not that one culture can't show another culture, it's about the intent and the accuracy of the portrayal. Virtually all Westerns prior to 1950 have horrifically racist views of Native Americans, and we can all agree that this is wrong. By contrast there were just a few voices of dissent when *Killers of the Flower Moon* came out in 2023. Some felt there was too much emphasis on the white man and that it wasn't respectful enough to the Osage people. For anyone who saw the Scorsese film it's hard to see where that argument is valid. Of the three main cast members one is Lily Gladstone, a woman with native people heritage, and the others are Hollywood royalty, Leonardo DiCaprio and Robert De Niro.

Do the critics seriously think that a $200 million budget and millions of filled theatre seats would have happened if the entire cast and crew were unknowns? The film is all about the plight of the Osage people and the abuse these people had inflicted on them. The white man is shown as a plague, not a civilising force for good. Movies have come a long way since *Cimarron*. Too often the complaints are being made by those using cultural appropriation as a weapon rather than looking at the meaning of the definition or the intent of a master filmmaker like Martin Scorsese.

In HR law the concept of "offence" is defined by the victim. "I didn't mean it that way" isn't a valid defence. This concept is being used in movies. Some will say, what right does a white man have to talk about racial diversity and cultural appropriation? I would politely ask people to look at my name: I live in Britain and Jem Duducu is not an Anglo-Saxon name. I'm the son of immigrants; neither of my parents were born on the continent where I live. I once heard the term "professionally offended" and there's a lot of that online. The problem is that many complainants appear to have nothing better to do but exaggerate the impact on the conversations around diversity, cultural appropriation and other complex and nuanced topics. This has led to the concept of the "lived experience": if it didn't happen to you, you do not have the right to portray it or write about it, but this concept falls at the first hurdle. Without imagination, no fantasy, no historical fiction and none of the films in this book would exist, and as I haven't directed a Western, this book has no right to exist either. If each ethnic group can write only about themselves, we are left only with siloed entertainment that doesn't reflect the wonderfully culturally and racially diverse populations that exist across the globe.

Going back to the original meaning of the term "cultural appropriation", yes, the film might have been made by a white guy, but if respect is shown, and effort and time have been spent to accurately portray another culture, it is not an example of cultural appropriation. But what about the white saviour? This is the idea that native peoples (in whatever context) can't conduct their own affairs or effectively resist until a white man turns up to show them how to do it. Obviously, this runs into the odious concept of racial superiority. In many films we see the white man help, but the best examples are those where the white man learns at least as much, if not more, from the native peoples than they learn from him. Again, to pretend that only indigenous cultures are good, and every aspect of Western culture is bad is just as racist as the other way around. To take away any people's agency and put it into the hands of another race or culture is unacceptable. There are times when this concept is fumbled and others where it is done magnificently. In the most careful hands, the white man isn't a saviour but the audience's way into something that is not every day; as he learns, we learn. Life, like history is complicated, and movies, because their first job is to entertain, need to simplify complicated issues.

With all of that in mind, let's take some tentative steps in the right direction with *A Man Called Horse*, a film whose heart is in the right place but doesn't stand the test of time. This 1970 movie starring Richard Harris has an intriguing and unusual premise. Like many of the worthier Westerns it's not an original script but is based on a short story also called A Man Called Horse by Dorothy M Johnson (who also wrote The Man Who Shot Liberty Valance). First published in a magazine in 1950, the story is that of a Victorian English aristocrat who wants to go to the last great frontier, the Wild West, and meet some of these native peoples he's read about - to see what kind of man he is. He meets a tribe of Sioux who have never seen a white man before (Harris is the palest of Europeans, and with his blonde hair, he must look like an albino to the average Sioux). Initially, they abuse and humiliate him and give him the name Horse because they see him as an animal and not a man. He eventually wins their trust and becomes a Sioux brave when he undergoes a brutal ritual, the most famous scene in the movie.

If there's one thing people today remember about the film (if it's remembered at all) it's when Richard Harris is suspended by hooks in his chest. Correct. It's the standout scene. Harris's face is wracked with pain and blood is trickling down his chest; it's an impressive prosthetic even by today's standards. Is it great cinema? Yes. Is it historically accurate? No. And so we get into the issue of cultural appropriation and sensitivity. In the film this supposed Sioux initiation ceremony is called the Vow to the Sun. This is wrong. The Sioux did have territory in the Dakotas, but so did another group called the Nueta, who were alleged to have a ritual called O-Kee-Pa (Buffalo Dance), which may have involved suspension from a tree or the rafters of a hut with pegs cut into the pectorals, described by the American painter George Catlin. However, that tribe was virtually wiped out by smallpox in 1837. This was before the events depicted in the movie; it also means that a white artist, the only person who recorded this, is not a reliable source of native ceremonies. The debate about whether this ritual existed still rages today, but even if it did, it certainly wasn't the Sioux who did it. The rule of cool always gets Hollywood in trouble when it's doing historical films. Does full-plate armour look cool? Yes. Should Charlton Heston be wearing it in *El Cid*? No, it's 300 years too early. Is the scene with Richard Harris being suspended by ropes torn into his flesh tense and dramatic? Yes. Could it have happened, and does it show the appropriate respect for the Sioux? No.

But the film is obviously trying. It's the first Western to spend time with native peoples and make them the protagonists, and it's the first to have scenes using the Sioux language. Most of the actors are of native ancestry, although the Sioux leaders are played by white actors in fake tan. And there's an interracial love scene. Running Deer is played by the Greek actress (and former Miss Universe) Corinna Tsopei, but she's made up to look like a native. While this was not the first film to show a caring, romantic relationship between a white man and a native woman, it was probably the most nuanced and mature one so far shown onscreen. Despite its flaws, *A Man Called Horse* was the perfect bridge between the old way of making Westerns and a new and enlightened way of portraying the complex societies of indigenous peoples.

While the white saviour elements are kept to a minimum for most of the film, they come crashing into the foreground at the end. By now Harris has been accepted as a warrior and a neighbouring tribe is set to attack, so using his white man tactics (form two ranks, etc.) he is able to lead the tribe to a great victory and - good news - he becomes the chief! A white guy is in charge, the world is back to the way it should be, roll credits. Okay, that's a little facetious, but after all their efforts to make something new, something that challenged the status quo, the filmmakers couldn't help themselves and resorted to a crushingly predictable, old-fashioned ending.

"They were of their time" is what critics say when reviewing sacred cows of the past that do not reflect modern societal norms. The reality is *A Man Called Horse* was not of its time, it was groundbreaking. It was more subversive and fresher than *McCabe & Mrs Miller*. Unfortunately, while it had taken a colossal leap in the right direction, it hadn't jumped far enough, but then again, what new art makes the transition successfully on the first go? The film was nominated for several awards, but not the Oscars, and while it did only mediocre business in America, it did great business globally. Eighty years after Buffalo Bill's Wild West show, the rest of the world still couldn't get enough of the exotica that was the Wild West, and as this was a new take on the same era, it was a bigger hit worldwide than *Paint Your Wagon* or *True Grit*. It would lead to two (inferior) sequels, both starring Harris.

Then there's John Wayne's last movie *The Shootist*, filmed in 1976. The story is about a tough sheriff who has killed thirty men throughout his long career and who now finds out he has terminal cancer. The year is 1901, so it's the death of the Old West and the death of a man who is a relic of that era. It was meant to be John Wayne's career farewell. By this time, he was sixty-nine and having been diagnosed with lung cancer in 1964, had undergone the surgical removal of his left lung and several ribs. He made a full recovery but spent the rest of his life with greatly reduced lung capacity (naturally). As a result, he had barely managed the filming of *Rooster Cogburn* and was seen as too frail to take on this latest role. But after multiple other actors, including Paul Newman and Clint Eastwood turned it down, he was approached and loved the idea. It is an urban legend that Wayne was dying from cancer at this time. He was not. An aggressive form of cancer later returned, and he died in 1979.

The Shootist was seen by Wayne, the filmmakers and the audiences as a fitting farewell to a career that had begun back into the silent era and went on to span more than fifty years. The film was directed by Don Siegel, famous for *Dirty Harry*, and came out in the same year as *Rocky*, *All the President's Men* and *The Omen*. All of this gives you an idea of how long Wayne's career had been.

Filming was shut down for a week while Wayne recovered from influenza, an incredibly dangerous condition for a man with only one lung, but he made a full recovery and there were no other delays. Ever the consummate professional, Wayne just got on with it. The scene where he finds out he has cancer he later said he played for real, and in retrospect, the film looks like it was tailor made for him; certainly, he elevated the whole movie. The point of the film is that the sheriff is looking for a more noble and less painful death than being devoured from the inside by cancer. He's an old man looking for trouble so he can be put out of his misery. Wayne had script approval and changed the ending. He wasn't going to have this film be the first time he shot a man in the back, and he wanted to be shot by the bartender because "no one could ever take John Wayne in a fair fight". The rewrites were a source of frustration for Siegel, but he had enormous respect for Wayne which, by this time, he had more than earned.

As a favour to his old friend, Jimmy Stewart came out of retirement for a role in this film. Stewart had retired because of hearing difficulties, and this led to a problem in the scene where Stewart (the doctor) is tending to Wayne. Stewart couldn't hear his queues, so these two Hollywood legends kept messing up the scene. Siegel eventually pleaded for the two men to do it better, to which Wayne replied, "If you want the scene done better, you'd better get yourself a couple of better actors".

Apart from these few bumps in the road, the filming was easy and everyone seemed to know they were creating a piece of cinematic punctuation that not only ended a career, but a Hollywood era. This is summarised in the opening montage which uses real clips from real Wayne movies of the past to reflect the journey that took his career from Hollywood's earliest days all the way to 1976. That opening montage couldn't have been done with Paul Newman or Clint Eastwood as neither then had careers long enough to show that passing of time.

The director, writer and movie encyclopaedia Quentin Tarantino wrote in 2020: "There's nothing in *The Shootist* you haven't seen done many times before and done better … but what you haven't seen before is a dying John Wayne give his last performance… *The Shootist* (is) not the classic it wants to be, but memorable nonetheless."

The movie was nominated for multiple awards, but nothing for Wayne. It came out to great reviews and did well at the box office. It wasn't a smash hit, but then again by 1976, Westerns weren't the sure-fire crowd pleaser that they had been a decade earlier.

The other notable Western that could be considered an attempt to grab an Oscar was *Heaven's Gate*. Directed by Michael Cimino, it began pre-production in the 70s. Cimino had first come to attention with the 1974's heist comedy *Thunderbolt and Lightfoot*, but it was 1978's *The Deer Hunter* that turned him into the hottest new director in town. At the time that was comparing him favourably to Spielberg, Scorsese and Coppola.

United Artists managed to bag the hottest director in Hollywood for his pet project, a Western, but not a cheap, violent Spaghetti Western. Cimino wanted to do for the Western what *The Godfather* had done for the gangster film. The film would be filled with great actors and give careful attention to historical detail in the clothing and sets. This would be a drama on an epic scale, guaranteed to get both the glowing reviews and the box office. The story revolves around the real 1892 Johnson County War in Wyoming. It was the ranchers versus the homesteaders, a fight used a number of times as background in previous Westerns, including *Shane*. Most of the characters in the film have the names of real people involved in this violent dispute, but the events shown are completely different. Also, while homesteaders did begin to settle in the area in the 1890s, there was no sea of unwashed, newly arrived Europeans killing cattle to feed their hungry families.

The original budget was a generous $11.6 million. The film attracted major talent, including Kris Kristofferson, Christopher Walken (hot off his Oscar win in Cimino's *The Deer Hunter*), John Hurt, Jeff Bridges and Sam Waterston. The French actress Isabelle Huppert was the love interest and with that budget, cast, director and script, everything should have worked.

Many books and articles have been written about *Heaven's Gate*, and if you've bought this book, you already know the film was a miserable failure that spelled the end for United Artists as an independent studio. But the writing was on the wall from the beginning. There's a famous urban legend that says by the sixth day of filming the project was already five days behind schedule. It's a great line, but the warning signs were there earlier than that. Before a single day's shooting, Cimino and his friends searched 20,000 miles of land looking for the perfect locations. That's not normal. Most of the town scenes were filmed in Montana, but filming also took place in Idaho. They might be neighbouring states, but Montana is huge, so why couldn't Cimino find or build something near the original location? Harvard University refused to be used in the filming, allegedly because of Cimino's excessive demands. So, rather than backing down or going to another American university, the prologue was shot at Oxford University, y'know, the one on another continent. And it wasn't just money that was a problem. The film became notorious for animal abuse because it included real cockfights and at least four horses died or had to be put down during filming. As a result, the outcry prompted the Screen Actors Guild and the Alliance of Motion Picture & Television Producers to contractually authorise the American Humane Association to monitor the use of all animals in all filmed media moving forwards.

In pre-production another infamous and hideously expensive incident occurred. When a frontier street was built to Cimino's precise specifications, he stared at it and declared that "it didn't look right", so it had to be torn down and rebuilt. The street apparently needed to be six feet wider. Sensibly, the set construction manager said it would be cheaper to tear down one side and move it back six feet, but Cimino insisted that both sides be dismantled and both sides moved back three feet, then reassembled. Due to Cimino's reputation as an auteur, a genius, should anyone have tried to restrain him in his work? The answer was yes. A similar situation had recently occurred with Francis Ford Coppola and his epically long and expensive shooting of *Apocalypse Now*. Cimino was given too much freedom, too much money and too much time to do everything he wanted, including burn through money to create a colossal piece of ego. United Artists had forgotten the second half of the phrase "show business".

The $11.6 million budget ballooned to a frankly ridiculous $44 million, making *Paint Your Wagon* look comparatively frugal. Filming went on for so long John Hurt was able to film the whole of *The Elephant Man* whilst still technically filming *Heaven's Gate*. So, what did United Artists get for all this indulgence of time, trouble and money? Well, they certainly had quantity. After a nearly a year of filming, Cimino had 220 hours of raw footage, more than Coppola had for *Apocalypse Now*.

Cimino locked himself (some say literally, although this is disputed) and the editor into an editing suite for three months to emerge, presumably blinking in the first sunlight he'd seen for a quarter of a year, to reveal a workprint that reportedly ran five hours and twenty-five minutes. Cimino said this was "about fifteen minutes longer than the final cut would be". United Artists' executives thought about firing Cimino but didn't. He was sent back into the editing suite and spent more than three months getting his monstrous baby down to a three hours and thirty-nine minutes theatrical release. Even though that version had superfluous scenes of a ball in Harvard and a roller skating fiddler. In for a penny, in for a pound. United spent over a million dollars advertising the film, and it was released, thankfully, with an interval (*Killers of the Flower Moon* is only ten minutes shorter, and you need to have a bladder of steel because there is no interval in that).

The critics hated it and after a very short run United pulled it from its localised release to wrangle the monstrous runtime down again. Finally, it received a general release in 1981, with a much diminished two hour and twenty-nine minutes theatrical cut. By then United had no more money to promote it, and to be fair to Cimino, to release what was in essence half the original version meant that the story was cut to ribbons with inexplicable time jumps and secondary plots never resolved. The critics still hated it, the buzz around Cimino had evaporated, and for a cost of $44 million before marketing and the final edit, less than 10% of that was recouped at the global box office.

Cimino's reputation never recovered. United had to be sold off, and needless to say, the film did not win any awards. Years later critics have reassessed the original three hours and thirty-nine minutes, saying it was beautifully shot, with great performances and on a scale rarely seen since the era of the sword-and-sandals epics. In short, it is a great film (although it won't be troubling other contenders in the top ten Greatest Westerns of all time), but it wasn't worth all the trauma that came with it. Further, had the studio been less intimidated by the director's reputation, it probably could have achieved the same level of quality without the ludicrous budget and chaos.

The 1980s were a lean decade for Westerns. Sci-fi, action and fantasy were the new kids in town, and they were filling the movie theatres, but there was one truly great Western filmed at the end of the decade. Kevin Costner had been in the industry for years before he got his big break in 1987's *The Untouchables*. From there he had a hot streak with well-reviewed films that were box office hits, including *No Way Out*, *Bull Durham* and *Field of Dreams*. But Costner had been looking for a way to make a Western and had been speaking to Michael Blake who had been working on a different kind of tale of the Old West. Blake couldn't sell his script, but the two men knew each other from when they had worked together in 1983, and Costner encouraged Blake to turn the script into a book, which once published, would get some heat they could use to turn it into a movie. So, a script was turned into a book, only to be turned back into a script again. This was a tortuous route to get to a film, and publishers were not wild about the book either. *Heaven's Gate* had cast such a long shadow over the industry in the 80s it was perceived wisdom that audiences didn't want to see cowboys. The book was finally published in paperback in 1988. The rights were purchased by Costner, with an eye to it being his directorial debut. It didn't help that Dances with Wolves was not exactly a catchy title.

The first problem was that nearly half the film would have to be subtitled in English because not only did no one outside of America speak the Lakota language, no one except native people in America spoke it either. After that, it had a complex bison hunting scene that would need practical effects' work, as well as a US Civil War battle, and all this was to be wrangled by a first-time director who also demanded final cut approval as part of the deal. In the end Costner had to reach out to the British company Majestic Films International, which then worked with the Anglo-French division of Pathé Films, to get financing. A deal was also struck with Orion to get North American distribution. Everyone saw this as a risky project, and no one wanted another *Heaven's Gate*. But once again, a little strangely, we get Britain involved in the story of a Western.

Filming was largely in South Dakota where all the sets were built. Language coaches were on hand to get the Lakota language rightish. The language is complex and has different words and grammar depending on whether the speaker is male or female. As the language coach was a woman, and the female version is simpler, she used it for everyone. Only fluent Lakota speakers can spot this deliberate error, but apparently it's hilarious to hear warrior braves talking like women. The bison hunt proved to be the most complex part of the shoot and took a month to film. All the native people were played by genuine

First Nation people, and his role made a star of Graham Greene who played Kicking Bird.

Costner proudly handed over a three hour and one minute cut. Not *Heaven's Gate* length, but in 1989/1990 films that were two hours and thirty minutes were considered long. That most British of composers John Barry wrote the score. At the time he was probably best known for his James Bond composition and the score for *Out of Africa*. Barry created a lush, sweeping soundscape that instantly became a classic movie score. The film was long and the story was one that hadn't exactly been filling movie theatres for a decade, but the quality of the craftsmanship was there for all to see.

To complete the transition from Native Americans being portrayed as pantomime villains to their rehabilitation as the genuine good guys, we have to look at *Dances with Wolves*. Kevin Costner both directed the movie and starred as Lieutenant Dunbar. The film starts during the US Civil War when Dunbar, a Union officer, has been wounded and wants to die in battle (the terror of seeing a surgeon in the 1800s was very real). Quite by accident, he instead rallies the Union side to an unexpected victory.

And now comes an opportunity to talk briefly about the history of medicine: From the late 1700s to the mid-1800s there was a type of medicine known as "heroic medicine". The idea was to shock the body into wellness. Patients might deliberately be given a powerful emetic, forcing a violent purge through repeated episodes of vomiting, to "get the sickness out of them". Or worse, they might be burned with acids applied to the skin to force the sickness away through pain. George Washington had to endure this in his final hours as doctors tried desperately to keep him alive. We now know they were needlessly torturing a dying man in his late 60s. In such circumstances, a visiting doctor could be your last, worst hope.

Then there was surgery. Doctors at the time understood that shock and blood loss could be fatal, so the removal of a limb for medical reasons had to be fast. One Scottish doctor, Robert Liston, working in London in the first half of the 19th century, was known as "the fastest knife in the West End". He could amputate a leg in two and a half minutes. (Side note: he's the only doctor to have a 300% mortality rate. He was removing the leg of a man who died, when he accidentally cut off the fingers of one of his assistants, who later died from infection, and as he was wielding his razor-sharp knives, he cut off the tails of a spectator's coat - in those days people would pay to watch operations - causing the man to have a heart attack. Some have cast doubt on this story, but it's there in the records of the time.) In the Victorian era of science and innovation, nobody knew about microbiology, and as such, cleanliness was regarded with suspicion. A surgeon did not clean his apron, thinking the dried blood proved he was experienced. Of course, now we know such practices were likely spreading infection.

With all that in mind, Lieutenant Dunbar would rather have died in battle than be butchered by a surgeon, but his heroics earned him a chance to go to the frontier "before it disappears". When he eventually arrives at Fort Sedgwick (a real frontier outpost in Colorado), he finds it deserted. But it's a long movie, so to cut to the important part of the film, he gets to know the local Lakota tribe and falls in love with a young woman, a captured white woman, who was taken as a girl. Eventually Dunbar turns his back on settler life, seeing the Lakota as the more civilised people and their way of life one that appeals to him.

Heaven's Gate had killed an entire studio, nobody went to see Westerns anymore, and they didn't win Best Picture Oscars (except for *Cimmaron* and that was back in 1931). But Kevin Costner proved everybody wrong: *Dances with Wolves* was the fourth highest-grossing film globally in 1990 and was nominated for twelve Oscars, winning seven, including Best Picture and Best Director. The film was not just a hit but a sensation. For example, when she was a teenager, my wife watched it so often with her mother and sister they could recite some of the Lakota dialogue word-for-word; that's three British women learning a North American tribal language, that's how powerful the film is. People clamoured for a sequel, but Costner knew that couldn't be done, so instead, a director's cut was released with over thirty minutes of additional footage. It sold well on home video.

Dances with Wolves looks authentic and started the trend for movies to have a historical consultant to give credibility to the project. Consultants had been around for decades (you may remember the earlier reference to 1960 when the two involved with *The Alamo* asked to have their names removed). I have done some work as a historical consultant and the emphasis is on the word "consultant". On one project most of what they showed me was good, but when I made some suggestions for simple changes that wouldn't have been expensive to fix, radio silence followed. Thank you for the payment, and I understand that if there is a scene that might make the consultant blanche, the director will pursue his vision, regardless. Today, if a movie set in a historical era plays too fast and loose with the historical record, that effort will not be rewarded with golden awards. Look at 2023's *Napoleon*.

Dances with Wolves has been criticised by some for having white saviour issues, and to that I say, watch the movie. Costner is not better than the Lakota; he is able to give them the perspective of the white man, but that is never shown to be better. They help him more than he helps them, and their way of life may be romanticised, but the film doesn't make the cultural mistakes of *A Man Called Horse*. When Hollywood understood that this old genre was making a massive comeback, it gave the green light to a slew of worthy projects. The *Last of the Mohicans* came out in 1992 to great reviews, and while the box office wasn't as big, it still did well. That story is set during the Seven Years' War in the mid-1700s when America was still a British colony, so is it a historical epic or a war film or a costume drama? Whatever genre it is, nobody calls it a Western even though, once again, Native Americans are front and centre as the heroes. However, one of the legends of the genre picked up on the trend, and in the same year *Last of the Mohicans* came out, so did *Unforgiven*, directed by and starring Clint Eastwood. The crazy thing about this movie before we even get into the making of it is that Eastwood looks OLD, and yet, more than thirty years after this movie,

Eastwood is still directing and occasionally appearing onscreen. His career has been remarkably long, but his contribution to the motion picture industry is, in retrospect, probably more important as a director rather than as an actor.

By 1992, Eastwood was a Hollywood living legend. He had been playing cowboys off and on for more than thirty years, so in a way, *Unforgiven* was the culmination of his career in the Western genre just as *The Shootist* was for John Wayne. Eastwood was saying goodbye to his career in Westerns, the man with no name was heading for retirement, but he had no time for the nostalgia of *The Shootist*. He was busy creating a revisionist Western.

The story of *Unforgiven* takes place in the aftermath of an attack on a sex worker when the other girls in the brothel seek revenge by putting a bounty on the head of the perpetrator. Meanwhile, ex-gunman William Munny has tried to put his past behind him, but his wife has just died, he has mouths to feed, and he is a terrible farmer. The bounty is a chance to earn some money, right some wrongs and help his family. It's telling that the story of the attack on the woman, while true, is exaggerated by the time it reaches Munny. This is Eastwood's way of saying that while the stories around the Wild West did happen, they have been exaggerated.

Much of what Eastwood wants to convey is contemplative on the topic of violence, Munny saying at one point, "It's a hell of a thing, killin' a man. Take away all he's got, and all he's ever gonna have." And later, "That's right. I've killed women and children. I've killed just about everything that walked or crawled at one time or another. And I'm here to kill you." Said in Eastwood's distinctive growl, you believe it.

A few disgruntled reviewers muttered about putting people of colour in white people's history and were unhappy with Morgan Freeman riding by Eastwood's side. Unfortunately, such comments have only become angrier in the era of the internet. So here are a few important facts to consider about the real situation on the frontiers: In reality, about 20% of cowboys were Black, many of them freed slaves looking to start a new life after the civil war. That story is rarely told, and a Black face is a rarity in any Western film in the first half of the 20th century. Woody Strode was often the only Black face in these movies, and he appeared in some classics although he rarely had much to do or say. And because horses were small and nutrition wasn't the best in the 19th century, most of the cowboys were short, so the two giants of cowboy movies, John Wayne and Clint Eastwood, both comfortably over six feet in real life, do not accurately portray the physique of a typical cowboy. But they are who we think of when we hear "cowboy", right?

The title is ambiguous: are the actions of Eastwood unforgiven, or are the actions of the assailants he is hunting unforgiven? Like the best movies, it allows the audience to make up its own mind. Eastwood may have starred, but he had other older actors play most of the key roles. Gene Hackman is the main antagonist. Richard Harris appears as a troublemaker, a far cry in quality and tone from his days in *A Man Called Horse*.

Unforgiven, like *Dances with Wolves*, was mainly interested in reassessing the legends of the Old West. There is no soaring music like that of *The Big Country;* instead, the score is dour, sombre, and like so many more modern films, it is lit with natural sources of light. Night-time is a time to fear because you can barely see your hand in front of your face - and that's in a saloon. The violence is brutal and sudden. No slow motion, no actions are reinforced with music. This feels like the real Wild West and it's full of mud, blood and regret. Nobody wants to live in this place, which means it's a pretty accurate portrayal of the desperation of frontier life.

Eastwood shows his interest is more in directing than acting with the final "Dedicated to Sergio and Don", referring to his directorial mentors, Sergio Leone and Don Siegel. The filming wasn't difficult. Hackman and Freeman had been doing this stuff for years, and everyone recognised this was something special as Eastwood was clearly saying goodbye to the role that had made him a star. The quality is there onscreen, beautifully shot and directed, with great talent both in front of and behind the camera.

Unforgiven grossed around $150 million worldwide, about ten times its budget. It was both a huge commercial and critical success, with none of the contemporary reviewers having a bad word to say about it. Eastwood would be Oscar-nominated for Best Director, Actor and Picture. He didn't get it for acting, so he had to be happy with winning the other two. Gene Hackman won Best Supporting Actor, and the film also won the Oscar for Best Film Editing. The success of *Unforgiven*, along with that a few years earlier of *Dances with Wolves*, meant that Westerns had been elevated from cheap action films that Hollywood churned out with little fanfare to prestige projects with Oscar potential.

A film that cashed in on this idea of the prestige Western was 1993's *Geronimo: an American Legend*. Like *Dances with Wolves* and *Last of the Mohicans*, this Western would focus on the native peoples. The film was directed by Walter Hill, a man not known for his award pretentions, but a man who always produced interesting projects - and not necessarily for a lot of money. He directed 1979's *The Warriors*, 1981's *Southern Comfort* and 1982's *48 hrs*. The difference here was that Hill knew his Old West history, and he had a real affinity for the story of the annihilation of the indigenous peoples. Other jobs he took for the paycheque, but *Geronimo* was a project he believed in, something he seemed to have been subconsciously preparing for over the years.

Filming was on location in Utah, Arizona and California. Hill knew what he wanted to do and had a reputation for fast work (which is how he was able to work with smaller budgets), but Jason Patric was a method actor who wanted to do take after take. Their differing artistic styles led to clashes on set, but not to John Ford levels of animosity. Hill filmed with a tobacco yellow filter, in his words, "to make it look like it could have been filmed 100 years ago" and shows his attention to detail. However, he did concentrate on the warlike nature of the Apache, and initially, the film was called The Geronimo War. The studio wanted something softer like *Dances with Wolves*, but Hill pointed out (correctly) that the Apache had a fearsome reputation, comparing them to the

Spartans, which while not a great comparison historically speaking, at least showed the studio what he was going for.

Wes Studi played the titular Geronimo. Of Cherokee ancestry he had already received great reviews for his role as the main native antagonist in *Last of the Mohicans*. But even in the 1990s, the studios would have preferred a better-known white star to play the role in makeup. However, in a practical if not particularly enlightened move, he received fourth billing under Jason Patric, Robert Duvall and Gene Hackman. With a generous budget ($35 million, only a little less than the budget for *Dances with Wolves* and *Unforgiven* combined), and a talented cast, everything seemed to be in place. But there were problems behind the camera with John Milius and Larry Gross who wrote the screenplay: Milius was known for his bombastic entertainment, and Gross had been a script writer on *48 hrs*, a great action comedy, but probably not the first choice for awards' consideration.

What was eventually produced was akin to a Western you probably could have seen in the 1950s, except for the obvious sensitivities towards the native peoples. Wes Studi grabbed the opportunity to play the doomed hero with both hands, and Gene Hackman never put in a bad performance in his life. There are some handsome set pieces in the film, but at no point does it feel like you're watching a historical re-enactment; it's more like a remake of *Fort Apache* shown from the other perspective.

The film opened to poor reviews and rapidly fell out of the charts. With an initial budget of $35 million, it grossed a total of only $18.6 million at the global box office. Hill blamed a TV mini-series about Geronimo that came out at the same time. While that cannot have helped, it doesn't explain the film's virtual silence on the international movie scene where tens of millions had paid to see *Dances with Wolves* and *Unforgiven*. Some critics wanted the film to have concentrated more on Geronimo and the Apache people (that's a fair comment considering the new name of the movie, but not fair if you consider Hill had made a film that looked at a conflict from both sides and thought it would have war in the title). The reality is it simply wasn't as good a movie as the other two. However, it did get an Oscar nomination for Best Sound ... which it lost to *Jurassic Park*, not a win that was in any way controversial.

Hollywood gave the green light to more prestige Westerns, and in one case, it was a race to see who could tell the story of Wyatt Earp first. Would it be Kevin Costner or Kurt Russell? The Kurt Russell project that would eventually become 1993's *Tombstone* was a more populist affair than 1994's *Wyatt Earp*. On the one hand *Wyatt Earp* wound up getting an Oscar nomination for Best Cinematography although it lost out to Janusz Kaminski who worked on *Schindler's List*. On the other hand, *Tombstone* was nominated for two MTV Movie Awards: Val Kilmer was up for both, one for Best Male Performance and the other for Most Desirable Male, but he lost out to William Baldwin for *Sliver* (the mid-90s were a weird time).

While *Tombstone* was not designed as Oscar bait the fact that these two productions on the same subject were going on virtually simultaneously makes them fascinating to compare: *Tombstone* was directed by George P Cosmatos and written by Kevin Jarre. Kurt Russell was Wyatt Earp and Val Kilmer was Doc Holliday. The film was supposed to be Kevin Jarre's debut as director, but it soon became apparent that the project was too big for him, and he was fired. Cosmatos went in a different direction to the original tone and Jarre's screenplay, or did he? Kurt Russell later revealed that he took over both direction and script duties and that Cosmatos was a ghost director. Kilmer agreed with Russell, but others say it was still Cosmatos' show although Russell was clearly doing more than just acting. Whoever was calling the shots, the film became far more focussed on historical accuracy, getting the costumes, weapons and even facial hair right for the time (that's everyone's real facial fuzz except for the Sheriff, who had to come from another movie clean shaven). Val Kilmer worked hard on his quick-draw and his accent. With clashing egos and an ever-changing script, the shoot was chaotic, which is not a recipe for success.

The acting talent was a mishmash. Harry Carey Jr. (son of Harry Carey from chapter 2) was in it along with popular actors of the time, including

Sam Elliott, Bill Paxton, Michael Biehn and Billy Bob Thornton. Glen Wyatt Earp, fifth cousin of the original, had a cameo role as did Hollywood royalty Charlton Heston. All of that along with a voiceover by Robert Mitchum meant the movie was pulling from decades of Hollywood Western heritage as well as the law man's actual family.

Let's compare these two films: *Wyatt Earp* was directed by Lawrence Kasdan and written by Dan Gordon and Lawrence Kasdan (he also co-wrote *The Empire Strikes Back* and *Raiders of the Lost Ark*). As well as Kevin Costner in the title role, the film was packed with other stars including Gene Hackman, Michael Madsen, Bill Pullman, Isabella Rossellini and Tom Sizemore. This time Doc Holliday was played by Dennis Quaid.

Costner had originally been cast as Earp in the pre-production of *Tombstone* but disagreed with the emphasis of that film on the ensemble cast; he wanted it to focus on Earp. By contrast, Kasdan's original plan had been to make a six-part mini-series, but with Costner onboard, the project was repurposed into a film.

As both productions needed era appropriate costumes, more were brought over from Europe. However, unlike *Tombstone*, *Wyatt Earp* had his real pistol, loaned by the Earp Museum and used in some scenes during a number of close-ups. The film was released at three hours and eleven minutes, a full hour longer than *Tombstone*.

From this point on, the comparisons become much more interesting. *Tombstone* came out to generally positive reviews, mostly three out of five-star reviews. An entertaining modern Western was the general consensus. When *Wyatt Earp* came out, the reviews were harsher. It was well directed and well-acted but too long. It was too short to tell his whole life story, but as it was his mid-life that was of interest, the film was still too long. *Tombstone* cost $25 million and grossed just over $73 million, so it made a profit on theatrical release. *Wyatt Earp* by comparison cost $63 million and brought in nearly $56 million, making it a financial failure. I saw both in the cinema and was more excited by *Wyatt Earp* (who wouldn't be after seeing Costner in *Dances with Wolves*), which was clearly the classier of the two films. That said, Costner forgot one of the key ingredients of movie making: entertain your audience. He completely lost the plot with 1995's *Waterworld* and 1997's *The Postman*. At this point, the studio stopped giving him control of large budgets and vanity projects, but he will have his redemption in a later chapter.

After this, it started to look as if *Dances with Wolves* and *Unforgiven* were exceptions to the rule. The reality was there was nobody in Hollywood who could say goodbye to their alter ego in a way so closely associated with the genre other than Clint Eastwood. And *Dances with Wolves* had highlighted the plight of native peoples so effectively that anything else coming out just a few years later would pale in comparison. It was time to forego the slavish attachments to the tropes of the genre; it was time to become playful and truly innovative with the Western.

Chapter 6

Post Modernism in the 1800s

By now it's obvious what components are needed to make a good Western. The problem at this point was that so many had been made and referenced they started to blend into one another. So, if that was an issue for the writer, imagine what it was like for moviemakers. The solution? Change the components, break the rules or reference the tropes. Slide the concept inside a new genre. Let's get creative, there are no bad ideas: 3…2…1…Go!

Let's start with 1970's *El Topo,* a film that can be best described using a technical moviemaking term, bat-shit crazy. It is an early example of a film that's still definitely a Western, but you've never seen anything like it before. Written, directed, and starring Alejandro Jodorowsky, this Chilean French filmmaker is a master of surrealist, avant-garde films. Well, less film, more visual mood poems.

A stranger rides into town, gunfights ensue, and a bittersweet ending wraps things up. So far so normal, but that's about it for normal. Trying to summarise the plot would be missing the point; the film is about the experience, with wild imagery and nonsensical moments; it's not about narrative coherence. Lots of people die, a naked boy wanders around, there is plenty of Christian and Eastern religious iconography. If you've never seen Jodorowsky's work, this will be a revelation, possibly a confusing one. What is very troubling is the rape scene, which at the time he said was conducted for real. Sexual assault is a crime, it is not art. His comments in the interview were graphic and deeply misogynistic. Since the rise of the #MeToo movement, he has walked back his comments, saying that they were exaggerated to sell the movie. True or not, it shouldn't take fifty years to clarify deeply offensive comments.

Putting aside the possible crimes committed in the making of this movie - and that's asking a lot - Jodorowsky has produced something that is incredibly surreal, and while its influences come more from Dali than *Django*, if you squint you can see it's still a Western.

El Topo was always aimed at the arthouse, so let's look at something far more mainstream but just as refreshingly different from the usual Western, 1973's *Westworld*. Michael Crichton, hot off *The Andromeda Strain*, was first a writer and then a director of sci-fi movies and created some of the most successful franchises of all time, including *Jurassic Park*. The idea is that in the future people will go to Westworld in the same way they go to Disney World today. Westworld is an Old West town where all the occupants are lifelike robots. So, you can have shootouts knowing the robots can't harm you, but you can gun them down. The brothels are also popular. In other words, for everyone in the movie audiences who grew up on Westerns, this would be a dream come true. For a younger audience, a more appropriate "world" might be one with superheroes, and a real Westworld would do business only for the over 60s. The film even admits this by also having an Ancient Roman world as well as a medieval one in the background. The main gun-slinging enemy robot is played by Yul Brynner, inspired casting; after years of playing a cowboy, he could well be the face you would base your robot on. After the audience is introduced to this high-concept theme park, the Yul Brynner bot malfunctions and goes on a killing spree.

So, it is Michael Crichton who created the indestructible human-looking android impervious to pain that will mercilessly hunt you down, not James Cameron with 1984's *The Terminator*. It is a brilliant conceit that has its cake and eats it too. The sci-fi nature of the setting means the rules can change whenever it wants, but at the same time, the film has to lean into the Western tropes to make the theme park feel like the theme it's emulating. Richard Benjamin, who played the protagonist, summarised the attraction of the concept perfectly: "It probably was the only way I was ever going to get into a Western … So, you get to do stuff that's like you're twelve years old. All the reasons you went to the movies in the first place."

Westworld was easy to shoot; there were plenty of Western sets and locations looking for business as interest in the genre was slowing down. The film was made for just over $1 million and took only a month to shoot. The result was a movie that grossed over $10 million. It was so successful that it led to a sequel, a TV series and a much later rebooted TV series (which will be explored in the next chapter).

El Topo was never meant to be a commercial hit; it had "cult following" written all over it, but Michael Crichton wanted to make big screen crowd pleasers, and that's exactly what he did again with *Westworld*.

If sci-fi can skewer Western cliches, why not satirical comedy? Step forward Mel Brooks with his classic 1974 comedy *Blazing Saddles*. Brooks had already spoofed the world of theatre and musicals with his breakout hit *The Producers* in 1967. Why not try it again with a genre even more people can relate to. His team of writers, including Richard Pryor, came up with a biting social commentary around the story of a Black man who becomes the sheriff of a backwater town. The idea had already been in development by another of the writers, Andrew Bergman, but the project had never taken off. Brooks liked it, and now with a room full of writers, he was able to produce a distinctly crude screwball comedy.

As one of the script's writers and a standup legend in his own right, Brooks insisted Richard Pryor play Sheriff Bart, but the studio, claiming his history of drug arrests made him uninsurable, refused to consider him. The role of Sheriff Bart went to Cleavon Little, a serious actor who had largely been working on TV up to that point. Gene Wilder plays a washed-up gunslinger who is now a drunk (a suitable Western cliché). Wilder befriends Little, but compared to the more serious Bart, Wilder is the funny man who gets to summarise racial tensions in the Old West in a poignant yet comical way: "What did you expect? Welcome, sonny? Make yourself at home? Marry my daughter? You've got to remember that these are just simple farmers. These are people of the land, the common clay of the new West. You know ...morons."

Brooks was reunited with the fiercely funny Madeline Kahn who played the seductive show girl Lili Von Shtupp (a name that makes me smile as I'm typing it). She has a show-stopping musical routine (Brooks has always loved musicals) and a hilarious seduction scene with Little. Former NFL player Alex Karras has the small but scene-stealing role of Mongo, so it's not like there's only one source of jokes in the film. Arguably the funniest and most famous gag is what could be described as an ensemble joke which unfolds in the scene around the campfire with all the farting after the cowboys have eaten their beans.

The budget was a paltry $2.6 million, but the filming was easy and the production came in on time. When the studio executives watched the first cut, there was silence in the room. Brooks was worried he had fumbled the delivery. He had had serious pushback for his regular use of the n-word, but both Pryor and Little got that the point was to show the casual and sometimes venal racism that was inherent in America in the 1970s; if it was now being addressed and recognised in the 1970s, it certainly wasn't being addressed in the 1870s. Regular use of the n-word wasn't just an issue for studio execs, but also for Burton Gilliam (playing Lyle) and gave the actor real concerns. He genuinely liked Cleavon Little, and yet he was having regularly to use the very worst racial slur (which he never used off set) to a Black man's face. Finally, after several takes, Little took Gilliam aside and told him it was okay because these weren't his words, adding, "If I thought you would say those words to me in any other situation we'd go to fist city, but this is all fun. Don't worry about it". The executives also didn't like the seduction scene and thought the farting joke was just toilet humour with no merit. When Brooks screened the film to non-execs, they laughed virtually all the way through.

The studio nearly didn't release *Blazing Saddles*, fearing it was not only too rude and crude, but crucially, it might not be funny. They couldn't have been more wrong. The critics had a tough time with it, but as this wasn't meant to have artistic merit, calling the plot derivative was missing the point. The movie was designed to deliver a conveyor belt of jokes. If the audience didn't like the last one, there would be another one along in sixty seconds. Rather than having the wit of 1970s' Woody Allen, Brooks' sense of humour tended to be crude; it was a crowd pleaser, not high art. Worldwide the film grossed nearly $120 million, making it, somewhat ironically, the highest grossing Western of all time (a title that would pass later to *Dances with Wolves*).

While the jokes are vulgar and silly the whole film would not work unless the viewer was aware of the standard Westerns that had come before. If you were only half paying attention, you could be forgiven for thinking this was a remake of *Rio Bravo*. If you've never seen a Western, the film doesn't work. Mel Brooks didn't tell Frankie Laine that the theme song "Blazing Saddles" was for a comedy as he worried that Laine wouldn't sing it with conviction if he knew the truth. So, with the convincing veneer of a serious Western, with all the component parts they had, they could have shot a straight Western. The movie does collapse in on itself with the high concept that the film is a film. This is established right at the start when Little canters into shot as epic Western music plays over the scene, and the question as always is, where is the music coming from? The answer comes when Little rides past the band. But even big fans have to concede that the conceit of the film crashing into one film after another, while clever, means the movie has no real ending. The stakes evaporate when the film tells the audience the actors are actors. But again, to talk about narrative structure is missing the point, and that's the only thing *Blazing Saddles* has in common with *El Topo*. Almost as a joke in itself, in 2006, *Blazing Saddles* was deemed "culturally, historically, or aesthetically significant" by the Library of Congress and was chosen for preservation in the National Film Registry. I am not making this up.

Picture the scene: a stranger with a mysterious past rides into town. The bleached desert landscape shows that the townsfolk are just about clinging on in this arid environment. They are being attacked by outlaws, so the stranger reluctantly takes up arms and dishes out violent justice on the thugs. This is the basic setup and visual imagery of many Westerns, particularly Spaghetti Westerns. And yet it's also the setup of most of the *Mad Max* series of films. If you replace the cars with horses, what's the difference? The longevity of this series, marshalled under one director, is impressive. In 1979, George Miller directed a microbudget Australian exploitation flick called simply *Mad Max*, which turned out to be the first in a new series. *Mad Max 2* (known as *The Road Warrior* in the US market because the first one barely got a release) came out in 1981. Then Warner Bros co-produced *Mad Max Beyond Thunderdome*, which came out in 1985. A thirty-year gap ensued before *Mad Max: Fury Road* came out in 2015, followed most recently by *Furiosa: A Mad Max Saga* in 2024. That means that the series has lasted for forty-five years, and all the films have been directed by Miller (with George Ogilvie co-directing *Mad Max Beyond Thunderdome*).

There is a joke in film critic circles that says you can always sound smart if you say a film is fundamentally a Western. *Star Wars* … much of it takes place in a desert and a farm boy learns to be a fighter. Definitely a Western. While sometimes the critics may be taking the joke too far (*Star Wars* has many points of reference, Westerns being only one, but Kurosawa's *Hidden Fortress* is an even bigger one and that's set in feudal Japan), they have a point. The spinoff TV series *The Mandalorian* is more of a Western than the original *Star Wars*; it is more specifically a Spaghetti Western in space. Westerns are often simple tales of redemption or about not being able to run from your past. They are inherently good stories that draw the viewer in, so why not change horses to horsepower and put your villain in assless chaps?

The first *Mad Max* film is set in a near future (well as close to a near future as you could get in Australia in 1979, where all the money went on the cars); biker gangs have taken over the highways and society is crumbling. The authorities have created a new special pursuit response force to combat the gangs. Police officer Max Rockatansky has the worst time in the movie. When his partner Goose (the lesson from this film and *Top Gun* is do not become emotionally connected to a character with that name) is killed by the bikers, Max resigns from the force, distraught at the loss. When his wife and child are also killed by the gang, Max puts his uniform back on, grabs a gun and gets into his pursuit car, intent on revenge. It is not a hard sell to say this film is, at its core, a Western. His famous Interceptor car was a 1974 Ford Falcon XB. It's brightly coloured in the first film, but in the following movies it's a drab black or dull metal colour.

Filming that involves stunt work this dangerous, particularly on public highways, needs all kinds of permits and licences. This would have delayed production and cost money and would have required annoying things like health and safety and risk assessment procedures. Miller simply bypassed all that and carried out what he described as "guerilla filmmaking", fine for the makers of *Rocky* filming Stallone running down the streets of Philadelphia, but a very different story when filming a car chase involving half a dozen speeding vehicles on a public highway. The original actress playing Max's wife was injured in a chase sequence, so they had to replace her.

The filming was all so under the radar that the crew couldn't even use radios to coordinate the chases in case they interfered with police radios. However, as filming continued, the quite frankly casually negligent Victoria Police began to help the production by sealing off roads so they could shoot the scenes. At one point Miller panicked and quit but returned after a few days. Understandably, after a litany of dangerous choices, the crew had little faith in him or that the film would ever see the light of day.

Mad Max introduced the world to American-born but Australian-raised Mel Gibson. He was then only twenty-three and had appeared in just a few minor roles, including the period drama series *The Sullivans*, in which Gibson displayed the raw talent that would later fill movie theatres across the globe.

The production budget for *Mad Max* was around $400,000, but it grossed millions when it first came out; after years of home video and special re-releases or being part of box sets, it grossed $100 million worldwide, so of course there would be a sequel. It's only when we get to the second film that the whole world of *Mad Max* goes into overdrive crazy but also becomes influential. The start of the film explains there's now been a nuclear war, and the survivors are fighting for the few remaining resources. The first film had been influenced by scenes of anarchy during the oil strike of the 70s when fights broke out as people queued to fill up their cars. That becomes the driving force of the second one and all subsequent movies in the series. Now that there had been nuclear destruction Miller didn't have to film in towns anymore; instead, he could use the continent-sized outback to film for as long as he wanted, without the fear of hitting anything.

Costumes became fever dreams to rival *El Topo*. There is no logical reason for someone to wear American football shoulder pads or for Lord Humungus to wear an ice hockey goalie's mask, or the aforementioned assless chaps, plus face paints, feathers and skulls. The costume designers went wild, and yet this insane clothing has now become the standard for post-apocalyptic survivors now in media as diverse as *The SpongeBob Movie: Sponge Out of Water* or the tabletop/video game Necromunda. It's been spoofed in the likes of *Rick and Morty* and in so many other places. So, now we have Westerns influencing *Mad Max* which, in turn, starts to influence other media.

A final point on *Mad Max: Fury Road* is that it now provides a satisfyingly feminist take on the action genre (Furiosa became so popular she got her own spin-off movie). The resource gathering is still front and centre as a motivator, but the film is virtually one long chase. The familiar premise is that they have to keep moving as they head through enemy territory because they are under constant attack or at least the threat of it. Death-defying stunt work goes on around a big rig truck; it's a high-octane, pedal-to-the metal version of *Stagecoach*. The two films are structurally and tonally the same, just with a seventy-five-year gap between them, but there can be no doubt that the stunt work and cinematography have improved.

As the saying goes, there's no such thing as an original idea. We keep telling the same stories over and over, updating them for current audiences. The *Mad Max* franchise is the perfect example of this, and the movies are still thrilling audiences well into the 21st century.

Now let's take a look at the most "Western" of alternate meditations on the Western, 1985's *Pale Rider*. In this film a stranger, played by Clint Eastwood, rides into town and protects the innocent locals from the thugs of a corrupt mining company. You have read/seen this story countless times; indeed, it's not dissimilar to *High Plains Drifter*. *Pale Rider* has everything, including a definitive Western star and a setting in the Old West, with all expected iconography present and correct. So why is it in this chapter rather than the previous one? That's because the titular pale rider is a biblical reference to death, one of the Four Horsemen of the Apocalypse. Underneath his scarf he is wearing the dog collar of a preacher, and so this is a biblical morality tale or, at the very least, a supernatural Western.

While there are no visual effects that outright confirm this biblical take on the character it's subtly there. It's no accident that Eastwood's character doesn't have a name and is only known as the preacher. His naked torso reveals the scars of six bullet wounds that would have killed a normal man. There are references to the Bible scattered throughout the film. There are times he seems to be in the right place at the right time, ready to right a wrong even though, in the previous shot, he was nowhere to be seen. In the final gunfight he brings armed vengeance to the wrongdoers in circumstances where any normal man would have died. Many Western heroes have done exactly the same thing, but this time the allegories have been deliberately and thoughtfully turned up. The viewer can decide whether this is all coincidence or if the preacher is death riding on a horse.

When the film came out it caused quite a stir. *Heaven's Gate* had been so toxic studios just didn't make Westerns in the 1980s, but at the same time, this was the legendary Eastwood's first time in a Western since 1976's *The Outlaw Josey Wales*. People were hyped to see the man who rewrote the Western genre putting on a cowboy hat one last time - or so they assumed. The film had a very modest budget of just under $7 million, a reminder that if budgeted properly these movies could do the job for not a lot of money. It came out to excellent reviews and grossed a little over $41 million, making it the most successful Western of the 1980s at that point (it would be outdone in 1988 by the Brat-Pack-filled *Young Guns*, which grossed $56 million; its sequel in 1990 grossed $59 million and produced a hit song. These two Brat Pack films led to Westerns being cool with the teenagers of the 80s for a brief period). Virtually the only criticism was that this had all been done before … okay, without the supernatural angle, but Eastwood was the perfect man to both star in and direct this project.

Meanwhile, back to comedy, and in 1986, we got the brilliantly conceived and hilariously acted *Three Amigos!* It is another high-concept version of the Western where we are back in the days of the silent movie with Steve Martin, Chevy Chase and Martin Short playing three vain and spoilt silent movie stars who have had hit after hit with their three characters who together are the titular group. In the film a poor Mexican town is being attacked by outlaws and desperately needs help (so far so standard). The high concept comes in with the joke that the peasant villagers are huge fans of the *Three Amigos* movies but do not realise that they are make-believe and, thinking they are skilled gunmen, hire the actors to fight a real battle. The three actors have just fallen out with their studio and think that this would be the perfect opportunity to show the studio head that they are so in demand they are going to Mexico to do a film.

The magical realism in this film includes a singing bush and an invisible man. They exist purely for the sake of some great jokes even though they are not standard Western tropes. However, because the three actors are in no way equipped to deal with this dangerous situation, the ending is an incredibly wholesome one where the whole village works together to solve its problem rather than relying on the strangers who ride into town.

The film not only has moments for each of the comedy geniuses to do their own thing, but also has fun with the conventions of the genre, everything from the tough talking to how powerful real firearms are and the fact that poor and desperate outlaws are unlikely to know the word "plethora". Again, the success of the movie hangs on the fact that the audience has seen enough Westerns to understand the scenario and then laugh when it confounds expectations.

Let's return to sci-fi with *Back to the Future*, one of the greatest movie trilogies of all time. The same year *Pale Rider* came out, *Back to the Future* was released to become a global box office phenomenon. With one of the most bombastic and anthemic scores of all time, even just the little twinkle noise (all four seconds of it) is iconic. At the time, audiences were not used to multiple-part movie franchises; they existed but franchises were not the norm. So, at the end of the movie when Christopher Lloyd says, "Roads? Where we're going, we don't need roads," the DeLorean takes off and flies into the screen. Where are they going? Who knows? It's a way for filmmaker Robert Zemeckis to say to the audience, 'and they will continue to have adventures'. Or so people thought until, in the late 1980s, it was announced that the film would become a trilogy and parts two and three would be filmed back-to-back, again a real rarity at the time. Ironically, to keep costs down, Italian cinema had been doing this for decades, particularly with their cheap Spaghetti Westerns and the budget sword-and-sandals movies.

For the eight people on the planet who don't know the basic plot of the franchise, it's 1985, Michael J Fox has befriended a crazy scientist played by Christopher Lloyd, who invents a time machine which he fits into a DeLorean car. Fox travels back to 1955 where he runs into his parents who don't seem to get along, so if he can't get them to kiss at the enchantment-under-the-sea ball, he might never get to exist. As events unfold, he meets up with the younger Christopher Lloyd who helps him to travel back to 1985, hence Back to the Future.

The second film, which came out in 1989, picks up with the flying DeLorean, and they travel to the future of 2015, where they correctly predict video calls, but sadly, we are still waiting for hover boards and flying cars. However, family rival Biff recognises the DeLorean and travels back in time to 1955 with a list of sports statistics so he can make a fortune betting on future sporting events. Fox and Lloyd go back to 1985 and find it ruined by Biff (in an incredibly prescient spoof of Donald Trump), so they have to go all the way back to the same dance in 1955 to thwart old Biff from giving young Biff the sporting almanac. Everything goes well until, right at the end, Lloyd disappears in an accidental triggering of the time machine. Fox immediately receives a letter from a postal worker dated 1885. It's from Lloyd, telling him he has stashed the DeLorean so he can get back to 1985. End of movie two, which people complained ended on a cliffhanger, despite the fact that the first one had done so as well.

The third film, released in 1990, opens immediately after the second one ended because Fox reads a news story from 1885 and realises that Lloyd is going to be killed by Biff's outlaw ancestor, so Fox also decides to go back to 1885 - meaning the whole movie is set in the Wild West and this sci-fi series becomes a post-modern Western. And if you think that explanation is dense, I assure you it's only a summary; there's more going on than that.

Which film is the best of the three? That can be argued all day long, but the sheer genius is that number three is visually completely different to the other two. It is also incredibly metaphysical. If this was anyone's first-ever movie experience, with no other points of reference, they would be utterly confused. The film depends on the viewer having seen the other movies (naturally) and plays wonderfully with jokes you've already seen that are now running gags. But crucially, it also assumes the viewer has an understanding of and a familiarity with the Western genre.

When Fox travels back to the Old West, 1950s Lloyd takes the DeLorean to a drive-in movie theatre and tells him he has to get to 88 miles an hour to make the time jump and must do so before he hits the wall painted with a clichéd host of mounted Native Americans with Monument Valley in the background. In an exciting sequence he does just that and leaps into the past decades before the wall was built ("You're just not thinking fourth dimensionally!" Lloyd chides Fox). But as Fox lands in 1885, that host of Native Americans is coming at him for real – with Monument Valley in the background.

The film is a love letter to the entire Western genre. Every cliché is included and played with great warmth. Fox is dressed in what the 1950s think cowboys would wear, complete with tassels on the shirt sleeves. He's told he needs to change or will likely be shot. So, who does a kid from the 1980s dress like? Answer: the man with no name, complete with an identical poncho. When asked his name by the Wild West Biff, who is called Buford "Mad Dog" Tannen, this is what follows:

Tannen: What's your name, dude?

Fox: Uh, Mar ... Eastwood. Clint Eastwood (said with a confident sneer).

Tannen: What kind of stupid name is that?

Considering the Western had been all but exiled from movie screens for a decade, the film counted on people having seen Westerns on TV or at late-night screenings in the cinema. The films are smart, deliberately seeding the key points that would appear in the third film back in the second. The final shootout from *For a Few Dollars More* is on TV (in the Biff-is-now-Donald Trump version of 1985). So, when Fox pulls the same trick in the third film, even if the viewer hasn't seen the second of the Dollars Trilogy (which at the time was twenty-five years old), if they'd been paying attention in the previous film, they'd get it.

The respect is there on the screen. In a bar scene (which, of course, has the swinging doors and the spittoons) three old-timers get a few lines. All three of them are actors who between them had appeared in dozens of classic Westerns; one of the actors is Harry Carey Jr. and another, Dub Taylor, was in the *Wild Bunch*. You get the feeling that if Slim Pickens or George 'Gabby' Hayes were then still alive, they would have been alongside, propping up bar stools (although it's disappointing they didn't include Woody Strode).

The climax of the film is, of course, on a locomotive. Lloyd and Fox have to get the DeLorean up to 88 miles an hour, possible then only with a steam train. Circumstances force them to replay a scene from 1903's *The Great Train Robbery*. The following exchange takes place when they hijack a locomotive, scarves up around their faces, brandishing six-shooters:

> Engineer: Is this a holdup?
> Lloyd: It's a science experiment!

The ensuing chaos and near misses on the train are up there with Keaton's *The General*, which was filmed more than sixty years earlier and must have influenced the stunt team. All of this shows that Western DNA was coursing through this movie despite the fact it's sci-fi. Like its predecessors, the third film was a massive hit and the perfect conclusion to the series as well as a fun and a respectful salute to the Western genre.

Next we come to three movies which show groups underrepresented in films. As previously mentioned, 20% of the cowboys were Black, but where are the Black Westerns? The answer is 1993's *Posse*. After his 1991 directorial debut in *New Jack City*, Mario Van Peebles was hot. He was a good-looking African American who had just directed and starred in a movie tackling the crack epidemic sweeping America. It was glossier and higher concept than the likes of *Boyz n the Hood*, but it made a star of Wesley Snipes. More importantly, it made money, and the soundtrack, too, was a big hit and went platinum. *New Jack City* was a gangster film with a very 90s feel to it. So, when I heard his next film was going to be a Black Western, I was first in the queue. Imagine my profound disappointment when I saw the most god-awful vanity project of my entire cinema going life. I nearly walked out when Van Peebles caressed a naked woman with his gold-plated pistol (because women love the feel of cold metal on their bodies ... sure).

The budget was so tiny (about $3.5 million) that financially it did okay, but tellingly, at just $20 million the profit was less than half that of *New Jack City*. The film does make an attempt to tell a little African American history, highlighting the so-called Buffalo Soldier units, first created during the US Civil War, which were majority Black units. They still existed in 1898 (when the film was set) during the Spanish American War in Cuba. All this was quite noble, and the film is as handsomely shot as other Westerns. The problem is the posing. Van Peebles had starred opposite Eastwood in *Heartbreak Ridge*, and he's clearly emulating Eastwood here, it's just that Eastwood did it effortlessly and never to the detriment of a female character. In *Posse* Van Peebles acts like a cross between the man with no name and *Superfly* (a blaxploitation flick about a pimp) and that doesn't turn out to be a good combination. At the end, Woody Strode, playing an old Black cowboy, is interviewed talking about the importance of African American cowboys. He was the perfect man for the role as he had been playing Black cowboys for decades. *Posse* gets 10/10 for a fresh take on a tired genre, 10/10 for its social commentary, but a 3/10 for execution.

Now let's move away from the men and look at another underrepresented group in the Western genre, women. The first feminist Western was 1994's *Bad Girls* (the Will Smith/Martin Lawrence film *Bad Boys* came out in 1995). It starred Madeleine Stowe, Mary Stuart Masterson, Andie MacDowell and Drew Barrymore. The setup is an interesting one: the four women are working in a brothel when Masterson is assaulted by a customer and Stowe kills the man. It's a clear case of self-defence, but this is the 1800s, and a sex worker killing a man is not acceptable. As a result, the four narrowly avoid getting lynched by a mob and are chased across the wild frontier by Pinkerton detectives hired by the widow of the man who was killed.

Bad Girls is a more morally complex film than even the morally grey Spaghetti Westerns. The intention of the film was for female movie goers to get the same power fantasy that guys get watching Eastwood gun down a dozen men. This feminist film about female empowerment, starring four women, needed a woman to direct it. Tamra Davis was chosen, but three weeks into filming this wasn't working and Davis was fired. Jonathan Kaplan was brought in as director and the new script writer was also a man (so, two men replacing two women). Kaplan had directed *The Accused* and *Love Field*, both movies centred around female stories, so if you had to pick a man, he was the right one to direct a female- centric film.

Whatever his feminist credentials, Drew Barrymore threatened to quit the production when Davis was fired. The two women had become friends when Davis directed Barrymore in 1992's *Guncrazy*, but a contract had been signed and production had started, so Barrymore was locked in. She would later describe the experience as "the pits". The film didn't gel, and with all the disruptions, the budget rose from $15 million to $20 million, but it only grossed $23 million globally. Roger Ebert for Chicago Sun-Times summarised it best, writing, "What a good idea, to make a Western about four tough women. And what a sad movie."

There are plenty of motion pictures in this book that weren't loved by critics or weren't commercially successful at the time of release, only to be reassessed years later. *Bad Girls* is not one of those films. It was simply a missed opportunity, and the final product is unsatisfactory. This film has had no positive reassessment because there isn't a hidden gem to be found. It's not even so bad it's good, it's just a mediocre movie.

The third group in to be underrepresented in Westerns is the Hispanic community. It is worth remembering that the Spanish arrived in the New World before other Europeans and that the South American gaucho, the Hispanic version of the cowboy, existed long before the story of the American West. Which brings us to the resurrection of the long-dead *Zorro* franchise. The original fictional character was created in 1919 by Johnston McCulley. A popular character, Zorro appeared in dime novels, comics, serialised cinema shorts and so on. Zorro was a very early version of the superhero, with a secret base, a secret identity – he was the one who rights the wrongs. His calling card was his rapier, which he used to slash a Z onto people's clothing or into a door, and always with perfect precision; there was no gouging out chunks of flesh or leaving a less than perfect mark. Zorro is the Spanish for fox, and he had a fox-like cunning to his plans

In 1998, Zorro returned to the big screen with *The Mask of Zorro*, directed by Martin Campbell (a Kiwi who learned his trade in London). Now we have an older Zorro, played by that paragon of Hispanic sensibilities, Sir Anthony Hopkins and his daughter, played to smouldering perfection by the equally Welsh Catherine Zeta Jones, while the new Zorro was, thankfully, played by Antonio Banderas.

Martin had directed *Golden Eye*, the comeback movie of the Bond franchise a few years earlier, and he brought his signature dynamism, fun and wit to this film. It had a Latin (or should that be Welsh?) twist to the Western formula, combined with slick 90s' action. Hopkins brought the gravitas; Jones brought the sex appeal and Banderas sizzled in both the action scenes and the romantic ones. This was a classic Errol Flynn swashbuckler updated for the 90s. It is a sensational family film with all the trappings of a Western and so much more. Compared to the other films in this book, *The Mask of Zorro* was one of the biggest box office successes, grossing just over $250 million. The film proved that in the right hands, with a great script and cast, very old Western icons could match the action heroes of the day.

As a brief aside, all the lessons learned with *The Mask of Zorro* were forgotten a year later in *Wild Wild West*. Like a lot of 90s' big concept films this was a reboot of a 60s' TV show. The basic pitch was spies with gadgets but set in the 1800s; think a combination of James Bond and a cowboy (an idea so cool it will literally be done in the last chapter). This soulless CGI fest starring Will Smith should have been Smith's next big hit, but it lacked the fun, verve and wit of *The Mask of Zorro*. Instead of razor-sharp dialogue, we get racist barbs from Kenneth Branagh playing the villain and disabled jokes from Smith to Branagh, who plays a paraplegic. It was a thunderously expensive movie that didn't come close to other Smith blockbusters. It did produce an entertaining music video/single though.

Finally, to end the chapter and the 1990s, we come to 1995's *The Quick and the Dead*. It's a little like *Back to the Future Part III* and a little like *Pale Rider*. This movie assumes you are familiar with the genre and then has fun with it. Sharon Stone had been a hard-working actress for years. Appearing in such schlock as the love interest in *Police Academy 4: Citizens on Patrol* and Steven Seagal's *Above the Law*, her most prominent role was that of the deliciously vicious and sexy wife of Arnold Schwarzenegger in *Total Recall*. All that changed in 1992's *Basic Instinct*, when she brought back the 30s' femme fatale with such erotic vigour it is the role she will forever be remembered for, despite having been involved in much classier projects like Martin Scorsese's *Casino*. However, having shed her clothes to get Hollywood's attention she was keen to keep them on in future films, and as a very smart, independent woman she was attracted to the role of Ellen, the female gunslinger in *The Quick and the Dead*.

The cast was to die for. Not only was it packed full of reliable character actors who had worked with some of Hollywood's greats, but also some up-and-coming actors who would go on to become Oscar-winning megastars. Apart from Stone, there was (deep breath) Gene Hackman (who had only recently won the Oscar for *Unforgiven*), Russell Crowe (in his first role in an American movie and who was hand-picked by Stone), Leonardo DiCaprio (who the studio thought looked too young, so Stone personally paid his salary), Tobin Bell (who had a late career renaissance playing Jigsaw in the *Saw* franchise), Keith David (who is a reliable character actor in many great films), Lance Henriksen, Gary Sinise (hot off *Forrest Gump* although that movie had yet to be released at the time of filming, while his other project that year was *Apollo 13*), Mark Boone Junior (another character actor who always plays a scumbag) and Woody Strode in his very last role (he passed away before the release of the movie). If anything, this proves that Sharon Stone could have a second job as a casting agent.

The film was directed by Sam Raimi, who at this point in his career was best known for his low budget but highly entertaining horror films. The story is simplicity itself: there's a duelling tournament in a dusty frontier town, and gunslingers from all over the Old West are turning up to prove their mettle. It's *Enter the Dragon* or *Blood Sport* or a thousand other martial arts plots given a cowboy hat and a Colt Peacemaker. Of course, it turns out that whereas other entrants are doing it to heighten their reputations, Stone's character is doing it to get revenge on Hackman's evil sheriff who had killed her father. It's a genre mashup which, like the Spaghetti Western, has no interest in historical reality (nobody ran duelling tournaments like this in the 1800s). *The Quick and the Dead* was here to entertain and show the audience some cool but tense scenes.

Filming started in late 1993, delayed because Crowe had to finish another project in Australia. While making his own unique take on the Western, Raimi leaned into the heritage of the genre by filming at Old Tucson Studios, a location used for filming Westerns since the 1940s. Consequently, the background on this film had been seen in many movies over the previous fifty years. Thell Reed was brought on set to teach the gun-handling actors the art of the quick draw. Reed was both fast and highly accurate, able to draw, fire and hit a bullseye in less than half a second. He could also do tricks like spin a gun out of and back into the holster. He was the perfect man to turn killing into an art and a balletic display of skill, speed and elegance. Hackman played one of the oldest men in the tournament, but as he had the least amount of screen time, he got more practice than anyone else and was the fastest gun in the movie.

A love scene between Stone and Crowe was cut from the American version, but the rest of the world got to see a bit of skin. Living up to her confident, feminist image, Stone later said that the best onscreen kiss she ever had was with Crowe; by contrast, she said kissing Di Caprio was "like kissing an arm".

The film cost a modest $35 million but failed to capture the popular imagination in the way that the more highbrow, Oscar-winning Westerns of the 90s had done, and its box office was only $47 million worldwide. However, over the years, with various cast members and the director only becoming more famous, it has had a second lease of life in the home rental market.

Like *Back to the Future Part III*, if *The Quick and the Dead* was to be someone's very first movie, with no other points of reference, the film wouldn't make a lot of sense. It's a very modern looking movie emulating a time gone by but in such a hyper-stylised way it can't be real. The film only works if you love Westerns, but it's been ages since you've seen a new one. If you were to flip it around and send it back to the 1950s, the audience would recognise it as a Western but would be horrified at the sex and violence. It breaks almost every rule in the Hays Code and goes against the grain of a more patriarchal time when, unless the female lead was a woman from history (like Annie Oakley or Calamity Jane), audiences would not have bought the character played by Stone. Unlike its more worthy cousins of the 1990s, this Western's only purpose was to entertain, pure and simple. While it follows the conventions and the look of classic Westerns, it is, at the same time, giving it its own unique 90s' spin on things.

Chapter 7

The Big Country on the Small Screen

As has been mentioned, post-war TV was becoming an ever-increasing threat to movie theatres. Who could justify the expense of taking the whole family to the movies when you could entertain everyone at home for free? At first, all TV was live, but improved recording equipment meant filming on location was possible, and as the movie studios had known for decades, the great outdoors is not only free to film but looks great. This was one of the reasons why the Western took off, and the same would be true for the genre on the small screen.

America had the advantage of locations as well as mainstream interest in the genre. Filming Westerns in most other countries would have been impractical, so all the early TV Westerns were made in the USA. Made by NBC, *Hopalong Cassidy* was the first one and is an example of one of the earliest scripted TV shows in America. Clarence E Mulford created the titular character in 1904, and Cassidy appeared in short stories, novels, comics and even films. He was a big name by the 1940s and was an obvious, family-friendly choice for the studio to turn into a TV show. Cassidy's was a defining image of the cowboy in the 20th century. He wore a big, white ten-gallon hat, and he had a tough exterior that hid a heart of gold. He was always on the right side of the law.

Actor William Boyde had first played the character *Hop-a-Long Cassidy* (known affectionately as 'Hoppy') in a 1935 film, and so it was decided that he should star in the new TV show. Although the films had been waning in popularity, getting a movie actor, even a fading one, to be in a TV show was quite the coup. That's not to place the Hop-a-Long movies amongst the Western greats. They were the classic 'crank-'em-out to keep the kids happy' type of movie. In 1941 Boyd made ten in one year.

Now available and colourised on YouTube this piece of black-and-white, small-screen history has been preserved for the digital age. While it is important as the first of its kind, it's not a quality production, particularly when compared to movie standards, especially where the acting was concerned. William Boyd may have been playing a character whose shoes he'd inhabited for years, but it's hard to tell what's more wooden, the fenceposts or his acting. Most episodes consisted of Cassidy going from location to location to talk to people. This was not the era of movie-quality cinematography. Boyd was in his fifties, clearly out of shape and in no fit state to be doing stunts or fighting in rip roaring gun battles. Instead, there is, on average, one crushingly dull shootout per episode, only just enough action to call it a Western. And it is here we see the issue that plagued TV up until the dawn of the 21st century: there was big money for and from cinema, and TV was the poor relative. Everything on the small screen at this time was substandard when compared to what audiences could see on the big screen. *Fort Apache* had come out the year before this, and with the *Hopalong Cassidy* series in mind, it is easy to see why that film was considered to be such a great movie: quite simply, it runs rings around what was then on the small screen. However, that's looking at things from seventy-five years in the future, back then nobody had watched a Western at home before. There was nothing to compare it to, and it had a novelty factor that has no modern equivalence. Kids couldn't always see the latest Western at the movies, but if their parents or someone in the neighbourhood had a TV, they could watch every episode. Despite all the negatives, the show was a gigantic hit.

My favourite random fact, discovered when digging into this completely forgotten show which has no cultural resonance in the 21st century, is that the image of Hopalong Cassidy was the first-ever picture printed on a lunch box. Today, that is a standard form of merchandising, but back then it was a novel idea, and this new secondary revenue stream didn't come from a film but a Western TV show. Aladdin Industries, the manufacturers of the lunch boxes, saw their sales go from 50,000 units in one year to 600,000 units after they slapped Hopalong's face on their product. William Boyd made millions from starring in the show, merchandising and guest appearances, and that was in the 1950s.

Hopalong Cassidy ran from 1949 to 1952 over a multiple season run of fifty-two episodes. Why did it finish? For the first time in this book, we are not concerned with grosses or box office takings, but instead, we need to look at Nielsen National TV Ratings, the organisation responsible for independently measuring viewing numbers. The show ranked no. 7 in the 1949 Nielsen ratings, no. 9 in the 1950–1951 season and no. 28 in 1951–1952. In other words, the figures were telling the broadcasters that audiences had moved onto something else. Hopalong Cassidy's time had passed, but it was a great final hurrah for William Boyd who retired from acting after the show.

Hopalong Cassidy may have been first, but just months after the airing of its first episode, along came *The Lone Ranger*. Just like *Hopalong Cassidy*, this TV series had a cinematic origin, only this time, rather than feature films, the Lone Ranger character first appeared in a 1938 Republic film serial. The Lone Ranger is an altogether different character to that of Hopalong, and the opening scenes of the two TV shows couldn't be in greater contrast. As the bugle call of the William Tell overture plays, the Lone Ranger is seen in full gallop on his horse Silver, pulling out his pistol and blasting away before riding down a track bellowing his signature catch phrase, "Hi Ho Silver!" As the opening ends, we see him on the crest of a hill as his white horse rises on its hind legs. Even by today's standards it's exciting!

The premise of *The Lone Ranger* is much darker than *Hopalong Cassidy*. In the first episode, a group of six Texas Rangers are ambushed and shot. One survives and his wounds are tended to by a Native American called Tonto. The survivor asks Tonto to make him a mask and dig an empty sixth grave so it appears all six of the rangers have died. The "lone" surviving ranger and Tonto travel throughout the American West to help those threatened by outlaws.

With a masked hero fighting for justice, Republic Pictures created a Western superhero. A little like Superman in the early years, he didn't use his real name and is only ever referred to as "the ranger". Tonto was to the Lone Ranger what Robin was to Batman. Tonto calls him Ke-mo-sah-bee, the anglicised version of gimoozaabi, an Ojibwe word for "he who looks out in secret". Amazingly for the 1940s, Jay Silverheels, a Canadian of Mohawk heritage, was cast as Tonto, one of the first non-white faces to appear in a speaking role on American TV. *The Lone Ranger* almost immediately outstripped viewing figures for *Hopalong Cassidy*, lasting almost nine years with 221 episodes before it finished its run in 1957.

Thanks to the success of the TV Lone Ranger, the character went back into movie theatres, and more than fifty years later got a $200 million reboot from Disney in 2013. Disney once again missing the point that Westerns are low-budget affairs, the film starred Armie Hammer as the ranger and Johnny Depp as Tonto (Depp claims to have some native ancestry). The film is a well-directed action adventure, but as a sign of the times, nobody wanted to see a movie about a Western IP (Intellectual Property) that had been enjoyed by the new generation's grandparents. It flopped at the box office.

This seems like a good place to pause and tell the story of Bass Reeves, a man connected to the Lone Ranger and whose story is of special interest to modern readers. Reeves was a former slave who became the first Black deputy US marshal west of the Mississippi River, working mainly in the then so-called Indian territory. Reeves was born into slavery in Arkansas in 1838. When the American Civil War broke out, he was in his twenties, and when his master George Reeves left to join the Confederate States Army, he took Bass with him. What happened is vague, but at some point during the US Civil War, Bass gained his freedom, and as a freedman, he returned to Arkansas to set up a farm near Van Buren. He wasn't a great farmer but got a reprieve in 1875, when James F Fagan, the newly appointed US marshal for the region, was looking to hire 200 deputy marshals. Fagan had heard about Reeves and knew that he knew the territory (which included Arkansas) and could speak several native languages. Fagan recruited him as a deputy, a job Reeves held for thirty-two years. He earned his reputation as a well-respected lawman, bringing in more than 1,000 men to face justice, killing fourteen and even arresting his own son for the murder of his wife. When Oklahoma became a state in 1907, Reeves, then sixty-eight, had every reason to retire, but he became a police officer in the Muskogee Police Department, where he served for two years before he became ill and retired.

His is an amazing story and an example of the racial bias in America's retelling of its past because, had Reeves been white, there would have been numerous movies made about him. But he was Black so there weren't. However, sometimes there can be an overcorrection. As modern Black filmmakers are (quite rightly) eager to show the contributions African Americans have made throughout history, a theory has emerged that the Lone Ranger character is based on Bass Reeves. I think that is stretching a point: yes, they both worked with only a small number of people, they both worked in particularly lawless regions, and grasping at straws, they both rode horses and were involved in numerous shootouts, but the Lone Ranger specifics, such as the silver bullets, the fact that he was the lone survivor of a massacre, the catchphrase and the mask were all trappings of a fantasy. Reeves, the man, has come to the attention of the general public largely though Sidney Thompson's books, The Bass Reeves Trilogy, and Bass has become something of a cause célèbre. However, unlike the Lone Ranger, Reeves was real and had a complex life: he was married twice, and on one occasion he was arrested for shooting a posse's cook. Reeves said it was an accidental discharge while cleaning his gun. He was acquitted, but this was definitely not the sort of thing the Lone Ranger would do.

The Lone Ranger is an ideal, a hero dispensing justice, someone who never makes a mistake. Bass Reeves was a real man whose imperfections have been glossed over as he has become lionised - and why not? If White America can turn Wyatt Earp into a legendary figure, why can't Black America do the same thing? But even the mythological Bass Reeves falls short of the masked man who dispensed Hays Code-acceptable levels of justice on TV every week.

As the Reeves' story took off, he began to get mentions in movies and TV shows, and he appeared as a character in Netflix's 2021 movie *The Harder They Fall*. In 2023, Paramount+ devoted a whole show to his story, *Lawmen: Bass Reeves*. The format of the series (the clue is in the title), is that each one tells the story of an unknown lawman from the Old West. Series 1 went to Bass Reeves, played by David Oyelowo, who is magnificent in the title role. There's not a moment's slip of the accent from a man raised in South London to Nigerian parents.

The series covers his adult life from his time as a slave in the Confederate Army, to his career as a deputy marshal, to becoming a grizzled veteran lawman with one of the best (and historically accurate) moustaches in screen history. The only problem with this high-budget TV show is that in its attempt to bring Reeves to global attention it is so earnest that he ceases to be a three-dimensional human being. According to the series, Bass, a little ironically, becomes the perfect lawman - like the Lone Ranger – but with more blood and sex. This Bass never makes mistakes, and because he has no flaws, he isn't very interesting. Oyelowo looks great and sounds hard as nails; we know he can do complex character work, but that isn't here. An example: In episode three, he is ambushed by outlaws at night, and he fires seven shots into woodland in total darkness. Four shots are from his smooth-bore pistol; all four hit and kill a man. When he switches to his rifle, he shoots the last man three times, scoring three hits. All of this takes place in pitch-black night, with 19th century firearms and no night-vision goggles. It's a gritty Western that has entered the realms of John Wick.

The show has been a huge hit, the single biggest driver of subscriptions to Paramount+ in 2023. It shows that even in the 21st century Westerns can be popular and, currently, are more likely found on the small screen than on the big one. Indeed, Paramount+, as we shall see later, seems to be dependent on the Western genre to give them a fighting chance in the 21st century streaming wars.

In our look at the Western we have not yet had much to say about the role of radio. Going back to the era of *Hopalong Cassidy*, it should be noted that radio dramas were hugely popular from the 30s into the 50s, the era when virtually no TVs existed. However, as the new technology with picture and sound became cheaper, the era of radio dramas faded away to a very niche market. The advantage of radio was that entertainment could be about anything; only actors and sound effects were needed to create the appropriate atmosphere. Superman had a series, and there were lots of police procedurals. The *Gunsmoke* series started on radio in 1952 and continued until 1961. It became a TV show in 1955 and lasted well into the era of colour TV before ending in 1975. All the original radio characters were recast for TV as they would by then have been too old or simply unsuited to the new medium; it was easier to have the same setting and characters, but with different talent.

The *Gunsmoke* radio show was aimed squarely at an adult audience, with references to scalping, opium dens and even downbeat endings where justice didn't prevail, reminding listeners that *The Lone Ranger* was fiction, and sometimes in the real world the bad guys get away with it. Just as *The Lone Ranger* evolved from *Hopalong Cassidy*, so too, *Gunsmoke* evolved from family fare. Of course, kids also like (age appropriate) grit and blood, so the TV *Gunsmoke*, which was already well known and came with a built-in audience, was a smash hit.

The show was filmed in Ventura County, California, a location that was cheap, easily accessible from Los Angeles and had been used in innumerable low-budget Westerns. But of course, by 1975 the TV landscape had changed massively since its debut in the 1950s, not least by the advance to colour. When the studio decided not to renew the show, it did so without making any public announcement or informing the producers or cast members, so when the news finally emerged, everyone was stunned. According to James Arness, the star of the show, "We didn't do a final wrap-up show. We finished the 20th year, we all expected to go on for another season or two or three. The (network) never told anybody they were thinking of cancelling." It was an ignominious way to finish such a long-running series.

Looking again at the basic conceit of this book, Westerns have been instrumental in the development of all broadcast media but primarily that of the motion picture. Over the last six chapters it has become obvious how important Westerns were to movie studios, but now we are in the early days of television, and again we can see how producers and CEOs believe the schedule must have a hit Western. NBC had *Hopalong Cassidy*, ABC had *The Lone Ranger* and CBS had *Gunsmoke*; none of this was accidental. If one channel was winning the ratings war, what did other channels have to compete with it? In the 40s and 50s some of the biggest movies were Westerns, so it was not surprising that some of the biggest shows on TV would be in the same genre.

Two more early TV Westerns to consider are *Cheyenne* and *Rawhide*. *Cheyenne* started in 1955 and is less well known than *Rawhide*, but it is important because the series changed the TV format. It was the first hour-long Western and the first hour-long dramatic series of any kind to last more than one season. Double the length meant more complex stories could be told. Clint Walker played Cheyenne Bodie, a white man raised by Cheyenne, who travels the frontier righting wrongs. Walker was 6ft 6 inches tall and had served in the merchant marines, re-enlisting to serve during the Korean War. He was a big, tough guy, so playing a big, tough guy onscreen was hardly a stretch, but unlike William Boyd, Walker became quite the heart throb.

Walker went on strike for nearly a year over better terms in his contract (it's always about the money), but after returning to the series, he was still unhappy. He was now earning more than he ever had, but he was tired of playing the character and told reporters that he felt like "a caged animal". Maybe he wasn't quite as tough as initially thought. ABC's *Cheyenne* was never in the top ten of the Nielsen ratings, but it did well enough to last for seven seasons and showed all the channels that there was an appetite for longer form drama.

Rawhide started in 1959 and finished in 1965. This was another CBS hit. Set in the late 1860s, *Rawhide* was about the challenges faced by drovers (the real cowboys) on cattle drives. Like *Gunsmoke* (which was on the same channel during the same era), this was more mature fare, and like *Cheyenne*, it also was an hour-long drama, allowing for more interesting storylines. Due to the nature of the show much of it was shot on location, which meant it needed fewer sets compared to other shows. Topics like racism, addiction and even the fallout from the US Civil War were raised … in the Hays Code acceptable kind of way. But it was not the show itself that was important, it was its introduction of a theme song that was introduced via 1980's *The Blues Brothers* to a whole new generation and still recognisable to audiences who wouldn't be born for decades after the show went off air. Another, and some would say the far more important legacy of the series, was the introduction to the world of the tall guy playing second fiddle to Eric Fleming (who?), a young Clint Eastwood playing Rowdy Yates. Eastwood appeared in all 217 episodes and had even begun to break out with his Spaghetti Westerns before the series was over.

The list of TV Westerns is nearly as long as the list of American-made Western movies. In the 60s and 70s they were cranked out non-stop. Personal favourites for me growing up are the completely forgotten *The High Chaparral* (which has an amazing opening sequence and theme tune) and *Bonanza*. *The High Chaparral* had a pro-Latino message, with a number of the cast being of that heritage, particularly Henry Darrow who played the utterly charming but cheeky Manolito Montoya. *Bonanza* was a success for NBC, running from 1959, to 1973, giving it the same kind of longevity as *Gunsmoke*. The show followed the Cartwright family, whose head was the widowed Ben Cartwright, played with both patriarchal warmth and sternness by Lorne Greene. But I could just as easily be writing about *The Virginian* or *Maverick* (which was rebooted as a fun Jodie Foster, Mel Gibson 90's movie) or a dozen more that were hugely popular, long running and full of nostalgia for those who saw them (or the reruns) as kids.

And then there's a TV subgenre - the Western that turns up in a non-Western. Here are three very different examples that show how the heritage of this venerable genre emerges in apparently unrelated shows. The 1960s' *Star Trek* series was, for its time, one of the most expensive series on air. As such, to reduce the costs for sci-fi sets, Captain Kirk landed on a surprising number of alien planets that had old Earth settings, allowing them to use existing sets. Depending on the set, there were times when the actors on the alien planet had to dress up as 1920s' gangsters, space Nazis or, of course, cowboys. In one episode they even recreated their (completely inaccurate) version of the Gunfight at the OK Corral.

In season six of the British sci-fi comedy *Red Dwarf* the gang end up in a virtually simulated Western. All the characters portray the very icons seen hundreds of times in real Westerns. For example, the character Cat plays the Riviera Kid in a Mexican-style outfit. Every time his name is said there's guitar music and he dances, but he's such a master of the quick draw that he literally shoots incoming bullets out of the air. In this episode there's a duel, a bar room brawl and a drunk (robot) sheriff. All the expected tropes are included, and the writers are not only showing their affection for the genre but having fun with it at the same time.

Finally, in season two of the mega-hit comedy *Friends*, there's an episode where Joey is selling aftershave dressed as a cowboy all in white, when a new cowboy, dressed in black, arrives to promote a competing fragrance called Hombre. They have a showdown, with hilarious consequences, but by using the iconography and formatting of a Western they get more laughs out of the situation. What these examples show is that by now the Western has become so ingrained in pop culture that even referring to it out of context and in an unrelated setting, a TV show can get away with it because everyone knows what it is referencing.

Now, fast forwarding in time, let's take a look at the impact of HBO on TV. HBO is a cable channel which started by showing pay-per-view sporting events. As a cable channel it did not have the same restrictions on content that the national broadcasters such as NBC had, so when it launched *The Sopranos* in 1999, it caused a sensation. Suddenly the world saw what TV could do. Having hours to tell the story of Tony Soprano, the leader of a New Jersey crime family, we could see the subtle development not just of his character, but of all the characters around him. The violence was the bloodiest ever seen in a TV show, and there was swearing, sex and drugs. It was like 1970s' cinema had sneaked into the back of the TV and started doing its own thing. Prior to *The Sopranos* the best drama was on the big screen; after *The Sopranos* the best dramas were on TV as cinema became an ever more visual rollercoaster ride for tweens. Now production values for TV programming were as high as any for the movies. This was the start of TV's golden age.

While *The Sopranos* was still being made, HBO doubled down on the high-quality content and produced *Deadwood*. This was the Western made even bleaker than the likes of *McCabe & Mrs Miller* or *Unforgiven*. There was no compromise on the language; it's set in 1876, so the actors speak like they did in 1876. Where actors in other Westerns would simply say, "Tell me about your trip", the *Deadwood* version was "Elucidate me on the trials and tribulations of your sojourn". When my wife and I watched it, we frequently paused the episodes to discuss what was happening. This was a series that took no prisoners. It was also extremely graphic in its language and explicit in its scenes of violence and sex. Many actors made their names in the show, but the two who rose furthest after this series were Timothy Olyphant, who played the Sheriff Seth Bullock and Ian McShane, who played Al Swearengen (and boy, could Al swear), the owner of the Gem Saloon and in every practical sense the mayor of Deadwood. Olyphant would go on to be in the series *Justified* (more on that later) and appeared in Tarantino's *Once Upon a Time ... in Hollywood* (again, more on this later). Ian McShane, who had been appearing for years on British TV as somewhat sedate characters, started playing the hard man in movies. Even at age eighty he was still appearing as Winston in 2023's *John Wick 4*.

Looking at other *Deadwood* cast members, there needs to be a special shoutout for Robin Weigert who played Calamity Jane. For the first time we see Jane as she really was, a drunken mess. Weigert slurs her words and is borderline incomprehensible. Her Jane is not a hero of the West but a destitute addict to be pitied. She's just one of a dozen multilayered characters that sometimes you love and sometimes you loathe in this magnificent series, which is very much a revisionist Western. The tents are drafty, the buildings are roughhewn, and most people look cold, grimy and uncomfortable. The fabrics are coarse and the language even coarser. This is not a world you look at and wish you were there.

Deadwood was probably too ambitious, too shocking for the times. After three seasons and thirty-six episodes it was cancelled, with all the intricate characters and storylines left hanging. That was until 2019, when finally, the series got a TV movie and 110 minutes to wrap everything up. But more than a decade had passed onscreen as well as in real life and while it did an amazing job of giving fans closure, because the original series were so dense and complex, if you hadn't seen the series since it aired you would be completely lost.

Deadwood won seven Emmys over its run, and Ian McShane won a Golden Globe for Best Actor in a Television Drama Series. This is how far the mark of quality in TV Westerns had come from the era of *Hopalong Cassidy*.

TV was also the realm of the neo-Western. Back in 2010, Timothy Olyphant had starred in *Justified*, which ran for six seasons and a total of seventy-eight episodes. The series is based on Elmore Leonard's stories about Raylan Givens, an old-fashioned US Deputy Marshal (like Bass Reeves), enforcing his interpretation of the law in the Appalachian Mountain area of Kentucky. Most of the plots would work if the characters were dropped into the same location in 1880.

Olyphant has always had the sneer and rasp of Eastwood, and as he prowls around in his big, wide-brimmed cowboy hat, he is simply a cowboy from the Old West living in the wrong era. He carries a SIG Sauer P226, a Swiss-made semi-automatic handgun first produced in the 1980s and is the only thing about Raylan Givens that would be anachronistic if the setting travelled back to the 1880s.

When the pilot aired on FX in March 2010, it was watched by 4.2 million viewers and was the highest-rated debut show for FX since *The Shield* eight years earlier. The series got consistently high ratings and good reviews, but it finished after six seasons because Olyphant felt the character arc had reached its conclusion (although a seventh series had been planned), illustrating how much TV production had moved on since the time of Clint Walker whose contract made him feel like "a caged animal" in *Cheyenne*. *Justified* won two Emmys, which once again reinforced the novel idea that TV Westerns could be both popular and high-quality dramas at a time when the Western was no longer a common sight on the big screen.

But then, like a lot of things in life, after a period of time nostalgia crept in, and the past was viewed via rose-tinted glasses. The band got back together again in 2023 for the limited series, *Justified: City Primeval*. When it came out it received glowing reviews and was overall rated slightly higher than the original series. The week it hit streaming it was the number one show across all platforms. Unlike so many, this was a hugely successful comeback, so don't be surprised if more limited series turn up in the future - but that will happen only when Olyphant and the writers think they have something to say.

AMC, the company who at the time was on the hottest of hot runs with *The Walking Dead* and *Breaking Bad*, decided to create their own gritty, genre-redefining Western with 2011's *Hell on Wheels*. When the then little-known Anson Mount stood confidently in silhouette with a flaming background as the titles come up, another gruff legend was born.

Hell on Wheels is a quality drama where it is clear money was spent. Although not as cerebral or as shockingly raw as *Deadwood*, it was populist enough that the average viewer could understand what was being said even as characters were being gunned down in the blink of an eye.

Like most great Westerns, the main motivator is revenge. Mount plays Cullen Bohannon who had been on the Confederate side during the civil war; he surrendered and has only recently been demobilised. He joins the railroad to track down the Union soldiers who murdered his wife and son during the war, but he gets sucked into this great construction project, and in the process, he becomes first a foreman and later the chief engineer. The five series cover five years from 1865 to 1869.

The first person cast for the show was the rapper Common. He plays Elam Ferguson, an emancipated slave, so he has real issues with Mount when they first meet. Soon after, Dominique McElligott was hired to play Lily Bell. To be blunt Mount plays a pastiche of every Clint Eastwood onscreen cowboy. He's great at it, but his character has been a staple of the big screen for nearly fifty years by this time. It's Common and McElligott's characters who are the most innovative. Common's Ferguson may be free, but emancipation is not the same thing as acceptance, and he faces racial bias wherever he turns. McElligott is in a similar situation because as a widow she is now an independent woman in a man's world. Always underrated, she faces the same type of discrimination as Ferguson.

Hell on Wheels comes with social commentary, high production values, great plot lines and, just when everything gets a little too po-faced, a thrilling gunfight. To keep costs down the first four series were filmed in Alberta, Canada, and the third series faced disruption when the area suffered a flood. But apart from that everything went according to plan. The pilot got a 4.4 million viewership, which was the second highest debut after the first episode of *The Walking Dead*. It was a huge success for AMC but not with the critics, who ultimately saw it as a pastiche of modern concerns, a Spaghetti Western with high production values. They weren't wrong, but that's what modern audiences clearly wanted.

In 2016, it was back to HBO and back to *Westworld*, with a bleak and bloody view of the Michael Crichton original. The budget for season one's ten episodes was $88 million, and season two's rose to $107 million. This was TV on a truly cinematic scale. Oscar-worthy names from the movies were brought in, with Jeffrey Wright, Ed Harris, Thandiwe Newton, Tessa Thompson, James Marsden and Anthony Hopkins given roles. Then there were the up-and-coming talents such as Evan Rachel Wood, Luke Hemsworth, Angela Sarafyan, Aaron Paul (hot off *Breaking Bad*) and Rodrigo Santoro. With these extremely illustrious lists we have a brilliant cross section of the talent that HBO was able to attract. The executive producer was JJ Abrams who had just spent the last five years resurrecting both *Star Trek* and *Star Wars*, and the co-writer and producer was Jonathan Nolan, brother of Christopher, who together had written some of the most intelligent blockbusters in modern cinema.

The result was a TV show that eclipsed the original 1973 version in every possible way. Technology, of course, had moved on, both in front of and behind the camera, but that didn't account for the ambition, the intelligence and the twists. Both the futuristic and Western scenes were shot to movie level standards; you can almost feel the grit in your mouth as Ed Harris rides across the dusty plain. "It's not TV, it's HBO" was the slogan, and at this point in the company's trajectory, it seemed unassailable, not just because of the super ambitious nature of *Westworld*, but also because of shows like *The Sopranos*, *Band of Brothers* and *Game of Thrones* that preceded it.

At its peak *Westworld* scooped up seven Emmys; it won Saturn awards (specific to the sci-fi genre) and was one of the most viewed shows on HBO. It was at the centre of conversations, with viewers wondering what the maze motif was all about. What was the man-in-black's motivation? Was the intriguing Evan Rachel Wood's character breaking the bounds of her programming? Back in 2016, *Westworld* was more a topic of discussion than *The Handmaid's Tale*, *Better Call Saul* and *The Crown*. HBO had a huge hit on its hands.

The show maintained the original idea of the movie and kept the setting, but it lost the plot of a malfunctioning killer robot on the loose. Instead, it pointed out (reasonably) that maybe humans are the problem if they are paying to simulate murder and sexual debauchery. The Western iconography was front and centre in season one. In season two it was still there but blended with a feudal samurai setting which, if anything, made it even cooler. In the background Nolan and the other writers were pulling ideas from the 1980 TV show *Beyond Westworld*, which pointed out that life-like androids under central control could be the perfect spies, saboteurs or assassins. The action took place outside the theme park and became a techno-thriller. While the show's concept was interesting, it was too cerebral for TV audiences in 1980 and the show flopped. *Westworld's* new incarnation added a layer that asked if the robots were truly lifelike, could a human's memory be downloaded into it, making them immortal? As it turned out the departure from the theme park Western setting was the start of the problems in season three. It didn't feel like *Westworld* anymore. Where was the Old West? It now had more in common with *Blade Runner* which, while cool, was not exactly why people were tuning in.

This new, rebooted version of the show was so dense, so tightly packed with talent that as the laws of physics show, once a certain density is reached the sheer mass collapses in on itself and results in a blackhole. That's what happened with this series. Viewing numbers dropped dramatically, and HBO was paying a gigantic amount of money for a show that was no longer in the popular conversation nor a ratings' winner, so why bother? In 2022, after thirty-six episodes, it was cancelled.

In 2022 Amazon Prime and the BBC produced a six-episode revisionist Western called *The English*, starring Emily Blunt and Chaske Spencer. Like *Hell on Wheels* the choice of principal actors tells us that this won't be just another story of white guys glaring at each other in a gunfight. Blunt, who has made a career of playing highly capable women, plays the marvellously named Cornelia Locke. She is on a quest for revenge, but unlike male heroes who are invariably avenging a dead family member, her cause for justice is distinctly female in nature. As is the case in stories set in this time, because she is a woman she is continually underestimated and yet proves more than capable of getting out of tough situations, including shootouts.

Meanwhile, Chaske Spencer plays Eli Whipp, a Native American who had been a scout in the US cavalry. Like Blunt he faces intolerance wherever he goes. Spencer, like Eastwood, plays a taciturn hard man. The problem is that because he has to talk to Blunt, he's too chatty to be the strong, silent type but not animated enough to be engaging in his dialogue. Personally, I think this is very worthy attempt at a new take on the Western, and I'm a huge fan of the two leads, but it's the script and the plot holes that let it down. The two lead characters aren't together for large parts of the series, and yet the breathy opening makes you think there's going to be a romance that would make Romeo and Juliet look like platonic mates. Both leads are engaging on their own, but there is zero chemistry between them, and a plot twist explains why the relationship isn't consummated. So why have an opening where Blunt sounds like a lovesick teenager? Because Blunt has been ruthlessly pragmatic throughout the series, the final showdown between Blunt and her nemesis has no tension whatsoever; the villain has no cards to play to get out of the situation.

Real effort had been put into the making of the series (if not the script). It's magnificently shot, and there was a deliberate decision to shoot the exteriors in Almeria, Spain, where many of the Spaghetti Westerns had been filmed. The title credits have clearly been made by a design team that pored over the intros to the Dollars Trilogy and add a level of realism even if they are anachronistic to the 19th century.

To finish this chapter, we will look at not so much a series as a sensation that became a media platform, *Yellowstone*. The series was co-created by the ridiculously talented Taylor Sheridan who as well as being an actor, including a major role in *Sons of Anarchy*, and a director, also wrote both *Sicario* and *Hell or High Water;* the latter got him an Oscar nomination. As well as creating the spin-off shows from *Yellowstone*, he also created Sylvester Stallone's first TV show *King of Tulsa*, all for Paramount+ so producing some of the main draws and ratings' winners for that streaming service.

Yellowstone is the story of the Dutton family, the largest landowners in Montana, with a ranch about the same size as the state of Delaware, and their struggles as they face encroachment on their land by developers, gangs and the law. As far as the Duttons are concerned, there is only one law on their ranch, that of the patrician John Dutton, played to perfection by Kevin Costner. Set in the contemporary world, it's an example of another neo-Western. The hats, the horses, the cattle, the shootouts and the Indian reservation are all present and correct, but Costner is as likely to ride in a helicopter as he is to ride a horse.

The show is tonally inconsistent. Kelly Reilly plays Costner's daughter Beth Dutton. She is a drunken mess who can be a tiger in the sack with the next unsuspecting male, but when she's sober, she's a tiger in the boardroom, always one step ahead of the best lawyers. In an early scene she's in front of the ranch house, completely naked (tastefully, from behind), clutching a bottle of whisky; then she sits in a horse trough as if it's a bath. In the words of my wife, "I don't care how drunk you are, a woman would never stand around completely naked without trying to cover herself up".

The setup is like *Dallas*. It's boardroom intrigue and vying interests with a smattering of sex, drugs and rodeos ... except when it isn't. Luke Grimes plays Kayce Dutton, a son of Costner's who is estranged from his family. He doesn't like the overbearing power playing his father pulls, and after joining the army, has returned to settle down with a Native American woman with whom he has a mixed-race son. Kayce lives on the Indian reservation, but he gets sucked back into the family saga. In the first four episodes, seven people die by violence. So is this an action show or a family drama or a boardroom/business thriller? Good news: it's all of the above, so you certainly get your money's worth, but variety is not the same as quality, and it is jarring when scenes move from people in suits talking about the land registry to a nail-biting shootout. Most of the critics gave it mixed reviews. Everyone agrees that Costner was born to the play the role of John Dutton and Kelly Reilly is phenomenal, but the series doesn't quite know what it is. It's not serious enough to be a serious drama, and it's not action-packed enough to be an action show.

Yellowstone wasn't just a hit, it was a phenomenon. Looking more closely, it's the Western trappings that make it work. In an ever-changing world, with America becoming ever more divided, the nostalgia and sheer AMERICANESS of it all is reassuring. The iconography of the Old West is there onscreen all the time. Even men get branded in the series, and branding is AMERICAN (many other nations did it with cattle, but they don't have the Westerns to prove it). Cop dramas may change with the times, but there's no real difference between one set in New York or London or Berlin. Only America had the Wild West and that look instantly tells you which country you are in.

After five seasons Costner wanted out, but the show was such a ratings' winner it needed to keep going. The first plan was to go back in time. How did the Yellowstone ranch begin? We get the answer in the 2021-22 mini-series *1883*. Cleverly, the producers double down on the Western pedigree by getting Sam Elliott (an actor associated with cowboys) to play Shea Brennan, Tim McGraw (a famous country and Western singer) to play James Dutton and Faith Hill (one of the most successful female country singers of all time) to play Margaret Dutton. The show was a smash hit.

So, after testing the water with one spin-off, a new, ongoing series called *1923* started in 2022. It starred none other than the Oscar winning Helen Mirren and one of the most financially successful actors of all time, Harrison Ford (who hadn't been a regular in a TV show since finding fame with *Star Wars* in 1977).

The use of numbers grows. There's *6666*, about a ranch in Texas by that name that began regularly to appear from season three onwards. And there's *1944*, which will be a sequel to *1923* but without the expensive Mirren and Ford. There's also a planned continuation of the main story, potentially starring Matthew McConaughey. As with any series, at some point fans will switch off due either to saturation or a feeling of having seen it all before, but at the time of writing, the *Yellowstone* phenomenon looks bulletproof, which accounts for the endless variations of the original.

In the beginning, TV mirrored the motion picture industry, and the straightforward Westerns that appeared on the big screen also appeared on the small one. But as the decades passed and audiences' tastes matured, so too did the content produced by the national broadcasters and later, streaming services. Some were experimental or set in a new genre/time period; others were spoofs, and more were prestige projects designed to attract critical acclaim as well as viewing numbers. All of this is a sign that the Western, at least on the small screen, is in rude good health.

Chapter 8

A New Century, a New Take

In the 21st century viewers have choices like no other generation before. You can get your Westerns the old-fashioned way and go to the local cinema, or perhaps it's better to snuggle up on the sofa at home and watch something on Netflix. You can catch episodes of *Hopalong Cassidy* via YouTube on your phone on your way to work. The options for filmmakers are endless, and while the straight Western is a rare find in the 21st century, there are many variations that show the genre is doing well.

Let's start with two films in the style of classic Westerns and begin with 2003's *Open Range*. Following his increasing hubris in the 1990s, Kevin Costner gave the world an apology with *Open Range*. The film is an unapologetic retro Western. Budgeted at a very modest $22 million, Costner reined in his excesses and instead focused on creating a crowd-pleasing film which he both directed and starred in. The premise? A retired gunman is forced to return to his violent ways when he and his cowboys are threatened by a corrupt lawman. How many times have we seen that before? In a clever move, Costner hired Robert Duvall to play the kindly older man, a piece of classic Western casting in a modern movie. Michael Gambon plays the hissable villain Denton Baxter, and there is an early English language role for Diego Luna as Button. In modern movies women cannot be silent bystanders, and so Annette Bening is there to be a more than capable, independent woman not in her first flush of youth, but someone who has life experience and has clearly been through tough times before the film begins.

The story is nothing new, but it had been a generation since this sort of movie had been up on the big screen. Costner is not redefining cinema as he had done in *Dances with Wolves* nearly fifteen years earlier; instead, he's channelling the movies he saw growing up and audiences responded to it. Made with more care and skill than many Westerns of the 20th century, this one was simply a well-made movie done in the classic style. It received good (if not rave) reviews and grossed $68 million at the box office, so a financial success and a return to form for Costner.

The other straight Western of the early 2000s was a remake of 1957's *3:10 to Yuma*, which became 2007's *3:10 to Yuma*. The two central leads were the white-hot duo of Russell (*Gladiator*) Crowe and Christian (*Batman*) Bale. It was directed by James Mangold, who had done the highly underrated *Cop Land* and the Oscar-winning *Walk the Line*. This film coalesced some of the most exciting talents in Hollywood at the time and showed a real commitment to the source material. The unoriginal story (even as a remake) is that of a rancher (Bale) who agrees to hold a captured outlaw (Crowe). The two men have to wait for the titular train as the outlaw is being tried in Yuma. Crowe plays mind games with Bale as other gang members are coming either to rescue Crowe or kill him. It's a double game of cat and mouse, with the first round between the two leads and the other between the duo and the outlaws.

Like *Open Range* the casting is clever. Not only are there two megastars, but there's also Peter Fonda, part of the old guard of actors, who plays a role reminiscent of his father's terrifying villain in *Once Upon a Time in the West*. And there is the new talent with the ever-loveable Alan Tudyk and the always-interesting Gretchen Mol, who plays Bale's wife. James Mangold filmed the movie with the sun-bleached look of a Spaghetti Western but used the old *Bonanza* ranch to give the town of Bisbee, where the action takes place, a familiar and friendly look to it. The location used for the outlaws has a more dilapidated appearance to make it seem less welcoming. The film was bookended with difficulties. Unfortunately, on the first day of shooting a horse rode into a camera rig and was seriously injured, which meant it had to be put down. The American Humane Association investigated and found that a number of poor choices had led to an accident that was not the fault of the production team. At the other end, in the weekend before shooting was scheduled to wrap, a freak snowstorm deposited nearly two feet of snow on this allegedly drought-stricken Bisbee. Crew had to shovel snow from the buildings' balconies and roofs and distribute eighty-nine truck loads of dry soil on the ground to keep continuity.

Apart from that, filming went smoothly, but the film was rushed out because 2007 was to see a spate of Westerns, and Lionsgate wanted theirs to come out first. With a budget of around $50 million, it grossed $71 million at the box office, a long way off from what it needed to make for a theatrical profit. It did, however, get good reviews. Critics recognised that in the modern world they could take an old idea and go further with it, that they could be bloodier and more cynical. The two leads were acclaimed for their acting, and the film was nominated for a couple of Oscars. While it was a commercial failure, this was largely due to the production budget and is an example of how the remake can be superior to the original.

Both films could have been dropped into the movie theatres of 1969 and people would have recognised them for what they are, well-made pieces of Western cinema. The rest of the films in this chapter wouldn't be accepted in the same way. Two years before *3:10 to Yuma* in 2005, *Brokeback Mountain* arrived in the cinemas. Ang Lee is known for his beautiful and thoughtful movies that explore the human condition (and one garbage superhero movie *The Hulk*. Everyone has a bad day). So, when it was announced that Lee was going to do a film about two gay cowboys the conceit sounded like genius.

Lee hired two of the most exciting young male talents to play the leads, Jake Gyllenhaal and Heath Ledger. Personally, I think the film makes two inexcusable mistakes - and there's another that just annoys me. To get that one out of the way, let me point out that in a story about cowboys, there are … erm … no cows. The men are there to herd sheep; we have a word for that job and it's shepherd. So, there are no cowboys in this film, and I will admit that pointing this out makes me a pedant. But to its credit the story is an original one as there hadn't been a Hollywood movie about a homosexual relationship between two shepherds before.

The two bigger problems concern the setting and the structure. When I first heard of the concept, I thought it was brilliant. There is no greater symbol of heterosexual masculinity than the cowboy (except perhaps for the one in the Village People). Therefore, to explore how this façade can crumble when there are other elements involved could have been genius. So, let's talk first about the setting: where, in the 1860s, could two gay cowboys go and be accepted? The whole world would reject them. They would be forced to live a lie, snatching moments together on the open range before returning to their confused wives back on the ranch. It would be an achingly sad premise. But *Brokeback Mountain* is not set in the 1860s. For reasons best known to Ang Lee, the film is set in the 1960s. So, when these two men sigh that there is no place for them, I was almost screaming at them to get bus tickets to San Fransisco! I could have guaranteed them that two gay cowboys would have had a great time in that city in the 60s. This is not the story of doomed gay lovers but of two idiots who have never read a newspaper. I didn't have much sympathy for them.

As for the structure (spoiler alert for a film you've had two decades to watch), one of the men is killed in a hate crime. The other man was always the more highly introverted and taciturn of the two. This means that during the last 15/20 minutes we are left to follow the cinematic equivalent of a sedative; true to his character he holds all his feeling inside, which is powerful and painful but visually dull. *Brokeback Mountain* was filmed on the tiny budget of $14 million and globally grossed $178 million, making it a huge commercial success. It had strong reviews and won three Oscars. Clearly, my view of the film is in the minority.

Continuing in the contemporary world there is the tour de force of 2007's *No Country for Old Men*, directed by the Cohen brothers. A hunter, Josh Brolin, finds a case of money in the middle of the Badlands and decides to keep it, which leads to local gangs and an assassin hunting him down. The premise could be from a 1930s' movie set in the 1880s, but the setting is the 21st century and the amount is $2 million from a drug deal that went wrong. Chases are in trucks and cars, not with horses and stagecoaches. Tonally and visually, it is a Western, except it has the trademark Cohen brother quirks, and shootouts are with automatics rather than revolvers. The setting may be modern, but the idea and the filmmaking are old Hollywood.

The film is based on a 2005 novel of the same name by Cormac McCarthy which had good reviews and sold well. The movie was deliberately filmed in the southwest on the Mexican border (both north and south of it). Its nihilistic tone appealed to the Cohens who had used it in their previous movies, but this time they were channelling Sam Peckinpah who had created similarly grim, violent and nihilistic films using that same location. The brothers kept the very downbeat ending of the book, and it was such a rug pull that I know a number of people who were loving the movie right up until the last part that were so disappointed that it put them off ever watching it again.

The cast is a who's who of the time: Tommy Lee Jones is the lawman trying to make sense of the mess. Javier Bardem gets his breakout role as one of the most sinister villains in movie history (with one of the worst haircuts), and Josh Brolin is the man on the run with the money at the centre of the chaos. Kelly Macdonald plays his wife, a brilliantly complex mix of smart but vulnerable. Even Woody Harrelson turns up for good measure.

A lot of the action takes place at night, which gives the film a claustrophobic feel. While Brolin tries everything to stay one step ahead of Mexican cartel gunmen, Bardem patiently, unemotionally and methodically tracks him down, casually murdering on his way. Iconically, Bardem uses a shotgun with a suppressor on it. Suppressor is the technical term for what most people call a silencer, but the reality is they do not silence the shot, and those little pfft noises you hear in movies are pure Hollywood make believe. A suppressor can reduce the sound of the gunshot, but as a bullet breaks the speed of sound there is a crack and then the detonation of the gunpowder charge to fire the bullet in the first place. There's only so much a suppressor can do. So, they do exist and they make the gunshot quieter, reducing the distance the shot can be heard, but in the same room the shot would still be as loud as someone shouting. The suppressor on Bardem's shotgun is far too small, and the exit hole seems smaller than the barrel, so the firearm appears to be working by magic. All that said, it is an undeniably cool-looking and unique murder weapon. The film was made on a modest $25 million budget and grossed nearly $172 million globally, proving to be a massive hit.

The other big Western from 2007 was *The Assassination of Jesse James by the Coward Robert Ford* starring Brad Pitt as Jesse James. The title tells you literally everything about the movie. If you don't know anything about Jesse James coming into the film, you will at least know you will need to watch out for Robert Ford, played by Casey Affleck. Both the title and the production show the viewer that this isn't like your average Western. This one is more poetic, at times more a meditation on the mythological status of the Old West and the lionisation and apotheosis that turned these real men into legends. The pacing, tone and style of director Andrew Dominik is obviously taken from Terrence Malick, and the gorgeously bleak cinematography is by Roger Deakins, who could make a potato look so beautiful you would have tears in your eyes.

Those who got it, loved it. The slow pace and barren landscape were Dominik's point and intent. But for those who came to see a Western with Brad Pitt and got a ponderous two hours, forty minutes of men staring off into empty landscapes, it was a misunderstood disappointment. It was a critical darling that barely grossed half its modest $30 million budget and a classic example of a film to be admired rather than loved.

So, after the elegant beauty of *The Assassination of Jesse James by the Coward Robert Ford*, let's look at some big, dumb fun with 2011's *Cowboys & Aliens* – and in the space of that one sentence we can see the flexibility and diversity of the Western genre. And with this film we get a first for source material for a Western, a 2006 graphic novel of the same name by Scott Mitchell Rosenberg. Other stories may have come from dime novels, but nothing is quite as looked down upon as a medium as the comic book. The graphic novel has produced dozens of worthy creations that are not relevant to this book, but it's fair to say that *Cowboys & Aliens* was never going to challenge the likes of *Maus*, *Persepolis* or *Watchmen* in the intellectual stakes.

The story is simplicity itself: the year is 1873, and earth is being invaded by aliens. It's the standard fare of movies like *Independence Day* or *Invasion of the Body Snatchers*, set as they are in the contemporary modern world, but this is closer to the progenitor in *War of the Worlds*, which explored the idea of a vastly superior technology attacking Britain in the heart of its then gigantic empire at the end of the 19th century. Whereas H G Wells' novel raised thoughtful issues about how man abuses technology for his own selfish interests, any metacommentary is thrown out for whizzbang effects in the film.

Cowboys & Aliens stars Daniel Craig (at the height of his James Bond days) and Harrison Ford. The director was Jon Favreau who had just come from back-to-back *Iron Man* films, so he knew how to shoot special effects' heavy action. Favreau put more care and effort into a film with this name than would be expected, and there are various visual references harking back to the Old West. The easiest way to shoot it would have been digitally, but he wanted the movie to have an authentic Western feel, so had it shot on 35mm film stock. Location shooting was in New Mexico where so many films had been shot, and the stage work was done back in California.

As is the case with any movie needing substantial post-production VFX, this was an expensive film, (arguably one of the most expensive Westerns of all time). The budget came in at an eye-watering $163 million, but that was okay because everyone loved Westerns in 2011, right? And besides, the film starred James Bond and Indiana Jones; who wouldn't want to see that? The reality was that a global box office of nearly $175 million was massive for a Western, but it was not enough to turn a profit. In reality, it was an insane amount of money to spend on a genre that traditionally would be doing well if a movie grossed

$50-75 million in 2010 money. Plus, while the film is fun and Favreau's efforts are up there on the big screen, the name *Cowboys & Aliens* may tell you everything you need to know about the movie. Quite simply, it sounds dumber and cheaper than it actually is.

Which brings us to a trilogy of unrelated movies by Quentin Tarantino. In 2009 he released *Inglorious Basterds,* arguably his best work. He brought Christoph Waltz to the world's attention, and as he dominated the film in German, English, French and Italian, he picked up a Best Supporting Actor Oscar for his efforts. Tarantino brought him in again for his next film, and he was so good in *Django Unchained* he won the same award in 2013. That film was not one of the myriad of unofficial sequels to the original but a complete reboot. In the original, the blue-eyed Italian Franco Nero played the titular character; here he is played by Jamie Foxx. Nero gets a cameo (in English), which regularly happens in all reboots in any genre as a way of showing respect for past work, a passing of the baton to the next generation.

What Tarantino does with *Django Unchained* is to reimagine the Django character as a former slave looking for his wife (the gloriously named Broomhilda von Shaft, played with great dignity by Kerry Washington). She is still a slave to the utterly odious Calvin Candie, played with incredibly dark energy by Leonardo DiCaprio. Famously, in one scene, DiCaprio is performing an angry rant at the dinner table when he smashes a glass and cuts his hand for real. Di Caprio stays in character, but the other actors are visibly shocked as he uses his bloody hand for emphasis in the scene.

Tarantino alumnus Samuel L Jackson plays Stephen, the house slave who is wise to the ruse of Foxx and Waltz trying to get Washington back. Like Cassandra of Greek myth, he only speaks the truth, but nobody is listening. In earlier films Tarantino had been criticised for using the n word unnecessarily, particularly if he put it in the mouth of a white character for no good reason. The habit has not aged well, but in this case it is completely justified and contextually accurate. There is a great scene where a meeting of the Ku Klux Klan descends into an argument about how to make a good mask out of a pillowcase. They are portrayed as southern idiots. Tarantino is clearly an ally of the Black community, and the opening ten minutes, while greatly condensed, is a damning but accurate portrayal of the lot of Black slaves in the American South prior to emancipation. Because it's in the hands of a master director and screenwriter and because Tarantino also wants to entertain, he gets the message across to more people than more worthy works on the subject.

Tarantino gives African American audiences a power fantasy. DiCaprio's character is not dumb; he is a dangerous opponent who even kills Django's only white friend. When Django is outgunned and surrounded by hostile forces, DiCaprio's solution? Kill 'em all. The final gunfight on DiCaprio's plantation of "Candie Land" is far bloodier than anything seen in the original *Django*. The bodies are piled high and every gunshot wound is marked with a real squib. Like Favreau, Tarantino may have been making a modern film, but in a nod to the old ways they went old school on certain things: for Favreau, it was shooting on film; here, Tarantino used physical squibs (packets of fake blood that explode to create the effect of a gunshot wound), rather than CGI blood. When Django walks out of the mansion in the dark, wearing sunglasses, and framed by the complete destruction of the slave owner's house, there wasn't a movie theatre anywhere that didn't have a cheering audience, Black or White.

Leonardo DiCaprio, like other white actors, was uncomfortable with how horrible and explicitly racist his character was. However, Tarantino convinced him to be as menacing as possible, saying that if he didn't take it all the way, people would hold it against him forever. Even then, DiCaprio had to stop one scene because he was having "a difficult time" using so many racial slurs. Samuel L Jackson pulled him aside telling him, "… this is just another Tuesday for us". Some think it's DiCaprio's best performance.

Tarantino was known for doing low-budget crime thrillers, but *Django Unchained* turned out to be the biggest budget, longest shoot so far in his career, and at $100 million, the budget was not only a far cry from the original's budget, but also massive in comparison to most Westerns. In the end he needn't have worried as the film was a global smash, grossing $426 million. This beat the former highest-grossing Western of all time, *Dances with Wolves*, by about $2 million, although factoring in twenty-two years of inflation means that *Dances with Wolves* would still hold the title.

The score was Tarantino's usual hodgepodge of tunes from the past, but in this case, they were largely from old movies mixed with some new compositions, including both old and new work by Ennio Morricone, yet another nod to the heritage of the genre. *Django Unchained* won two Oscars, the previously mentioned Best Supporting Actor for Waltz and Best Screenplay for Tarantino, but the new Morricone song was not nominated.

After Tarantino had fun with that film, his next project was another Western, 2015's *The Hateful Eight*. The plot is even more straightforward this time around: it's the middle of winter, a bounty hunter and his prisoner find shelter in a cabin inhabited by a collection of nefarious characters. Tarantino brought together a rogue's gallery of great talent, some he'd worked with on many occasions before and others new to Tarantino's distinct moviemaking style. The cast included Kurt Russell, Jennifer Jason Leigh, Walton Goggins, Tim Roth (who got his breakout role in *Reservoir Dogs* but hadn't worked with Tarantino since *Pulp Fiction*), Michael Madsen and Bruce Dern. For the first time, Samuel L Jackson got top billing in a Tarantino movie. Tarantino explained that the idea of the movie was based on the TV shows of the previous chapter, saying, "Twice per season, those shows would have an episode where a bunch of outlaws would take ... hostage(s)...So, here's a thought: What if there was a movie with ... no heroes...Trap these guys together in a cabin, with a blizzard raging outside, give them guns, and see what happens."

Once again, Tarantino was reverential to the Westerns that had come before. Ennio Morricone composed a completely original score (although Tarantino claims he used some unused compositions from

The Thing, which also featured Kurt Russell being trapped inside a building, surrounded by snow), and real props from the era were used, most infamously, the guitar played by Jennifer Jason Leigh that was a highly valued antique from the 1870s, on loan from the Martin Guitar Museum and worth $40,000. At the end of the song, the script called for Kurt Russell to grab the guitar and smash it to pieces, so six replicas were made for the shoot and were supposed to be substituted for the real instrument in the smashing scene. However, Russell was not informed about any of this and destroyed the original guitar before anyone could stop him. Jennifer Jason Leigh's shocked reaction on screen is not acting. Understandably, the Martin Guitar Museum announced afterwards that it would never again loan guitars to film productions.

The Hateful Eight nearly didn't happen. During pre-production somebody released the script online and Tarantino was ready to throw in the towel; it was Samuel L Jackson who saved the day (once again) and convinced him to continue. Filming was largely on one set and had a substantially lower budget than *Django Unchained*. It cost around $60 million and grossed nearly $157 million, so it made money even though it's one of Tarantino's worst reviewed films. I noticed the problems while watching it. Most of his films are long, but they are long for a reason. In the case of *Pulp Fiction* every scene matters, and every scene intertwines with other scenes in the film. In *The Hateful Eight* there's a tiresome ten-minute opening sequence with a stagecoach; it's beautifully shot but the only point of it is horses are slower than cars and winter is cold. There's another extended scene around putting the horses away during a blizzard and then lighting torches to get from the stable to the main building. I thought this was foreshadowing something, but that was it; it's never referenced again.

This is the first Tarantino film that isn't as tight as a drum with the edit. This film was also the first time Tarantino mixed his own stories. While he had always been a movie magpie, so for example, taking from a Hong Kong film, mixing it with an obscure 1970s' Spaghetti Western, and setting it in modern Los Angeles was original, fresh and exciting.

In *The Hateful Eight* he is deliberately going back to *Reservoir Dogs*, and consequently, the ideas aren't as fresh as those in some of his other movies. Tarantino once said that having a room full of odious people means that you aren't rooting for anyone, and there's a reason why. In the old TV shows there would be a hero, someone like Michael Landon, tied up and held captive, so Landon is the good guy, his captors are the bad guys and you want his captors to die. In 1982's *The Thing* Kurt Russell and a team of scientists are trapped in a polar research base where an alien assumes the appearance of its victims. Who is the alien is a wonderfully paranoia-inducing conceit. *The Hateful Eight* appears to create a similar situation and asks who is the bad guy? Except here they are all bad guys, so it isn't the same. Nobody in the film is likeable, so you don't care who lives and who dies.

The title of Tarantino's 2019 film *Once Upon a Time…in Hollywood* plays on that of Sergio Leone's *Once Upon a Time in the West*. Leone used it again 1984's *Once Upon a Time in America* (a gangster movie), and versions of the title have been used in a myriad of other films, including the 2011 Turkish film *Once Upon a Time in Anatolia* and the 2003 Desperado sequel *Once Upon a Time in Mexico*. Tarantino used Once Upon a Time in Nazi-Occupied France in the introduction to 2009's *Inglorious Basterds*, and here it is again in this 2019 movie. The film itself is set largely in 1960s' Los Angeles, but again, Tarantino is taking the Hollywood past and repurposing it for a fresh, new look. Leonardo DiCaprio plays Rick Dalton, an actor who has made his name in TV Westerns. Tarantino's pop culture knowledge is so strong they shot the interviews Dalton does on set in exactly the same way these interviews were done back in the late 50s. Dalton's story is really the story of many actors in the latter half of this book. He had a decent B-movie tough guy career, but his reputation waned, so he went to Italy where he could make some money and revitalise his career in a bunch of Spaghetti Westerns. The film is almost a movie about Westerns rather than being one itself. Tarantino even films a scene where DiCaprio is playing Dalton who is now playing a villain doing a scene. As the camera and DiCaprio draw you in, you believe what you are seeing, so when Dalton jumps out of character to ask for a line you are suddenly shaken from the fiction that you are watching a movie within a movie. *Once Upon a Time ... in Hollywood* cost around $90 million but grossed over $377 million worldwide. It was Tarantino's second biggest hit after *Django Unchained*.

By the time Leonardo Di Caprio appeared in his second Tarantino film he had won an Oscar for 2015's *The Revenant*. Directed by Alejandro G Iñárritu this was a tour de force filmed mainly on location first in Canada, but then as the snow melted the entire production was relocated to Argentina. Set in the 1820s, it's the true story (or in Hollywood parlance, a story inspired by true events) of Hugh Glass who was one of a band of trappers but caught away from the main party during an attack by Arikara warriors before he was attacked by a grizzly bear and brutally mauled. The group, still being harassed by the Arikara, leave two men to tend to the dying Glass: Fitzgerald is a frontier veteran and Bridger is a teenager. When Fitzgerald and Bridger, fearing further native attacks, assume Glass is dead or close to death, they bury him in a shallow grave and head back to camp.

Unbelievably, Glass still has some fight left in him and crawls/hobbles his way through Indian territory back to camp. Because he sees Bridger as a gullible kid, Glass forgives him but hunts down Fitzgerald for leaving him for dead. Meanwhile, Fitzgerald has rejoined the army and Glass knows he would be in serious trouble for killing a soldier, so Glass confronts him to have his say and Fitzgerald apologises.

You see this all play out onscreen. Because it's the 1820s, we are in the era of the flintlock musket, so no revolvers or Winchesters here. Iñárritu gives Glass a son from a native woman, one he never had, but which allows the movie to talk about the poor treatment of native peoples (the hunt for a missing daughter of the local native tribe is also a fiction) and sets the story in winter (the real events took place in summer). Iñárritu makes Glass's life as miserable as possible to tell a tale of endurance and revenge. Of course, Fitzgerald not getting his just deserts is not a Hollywood ending, so in the film Tom Hardy plays Fitzgerald with amazing physicality, and the two men have a vicious showdown at the end.

This movie may take place in snow with muskets, but it's hard not to call it anything other than a Western. After all, both the true story and the Hollywood version start with a native attack and show how lethal bows and arrows truly are. The film ended up costing $135 million to make (due to the relocation of the shoot) but grossed an unprecedented $533 million at the box office and won three Oscars. It was both awards-worthy and an action film all in one. It is also one of the most beautifully shot films ever made.

In 2015, three Westerns worth reviewing came out: we've already discussed *The Hateful Eight* and *The Revenant*, but Kurt Russell starred in the third, *Bone Tomahawk*, which was something of a cult movie. The story takes place in the late 1800s when the local doctor (a woman) has been kidnapped by cave-dwelling cannibals, so the sheriff (Kurt Russel) takes a posse into the caves to rescue her. The film goes out of its way to say that Native Americans are not the enemy but are troglodytes. Steven Craig Zahler is known for his low budget but brutal films. He specialises in gritty thrillers with sadistic violence, and films like *Dragged Across Concrete* don't sound much like a family night out.

Bone Tomahawk was not meant to be a breakout success and it wasn't, but it is an ingenious film that merges the Western with the horror genre. There is no historical veracity to this movie (which makes it like most of the Westerns ever made); the point of the story and the setting is to get a bunch of unprepared and outclassed people into a realm where they can be attacked from any direction at any time. It's one of Zahler's best, and if you have the stomach and nerves for it, you will enjoy a taught and stressful film. Like *The Revenant* the film shows the flexibility of the Western genre: it can be Oscar-winning art or grind-house bloody thrills, with everything else in between.

Continuing the bizarre comparisons, we finish with three films that couldn't be more different. After the intensity of Zahler let's move on to a comedy and 2014's *A Million Ways to Die in the West*. Starring Seth MacFarlane, who also co-wrote and directed it, the film is a crass, silly romp through all the tropes of the Western genre. As the title tells us, the film's main conceit is that the Old West was a terrible place to live: a splinter could kill you from tetanus, there were dangerous rattle snakes, people were thrown from their horses, and of course, "people die at the fair". Like all comedies it either tickles your funny bone or it doesn't. Personally, I laughed a lot, and one of my sons ranks it as his favourite comedy. While the points it makes are exaggerated, they are historically accurate, right down to the idea that facial hair in the 1800s was a sign of manliness. But once again this is a movie that if it were the viewer's first ever Western, it would make no sense. *A Million Ways to Die in the West* depends on the audience having as much love for the genre as Seth Macfarlane clearly does. It is a celebration of 100 years of Westerns and a commentary on the dangerous nostalgia of "the olden days" mixed in with fart and pee jokes. It is also explicitly film literate with a reference to Christopher Lloyd's Doc in *Back to the Future Part III* and Jamie Foxx appearing in a cameo as an unnamed Django. And it has to be a first to get both those films in the same universe.

The complete opposite of the crude comedy shows just how far the genre has moved in over a century. 2021's *The Power of the Dog* is a movie that has some of the traditional elements, such as being based on a book of the same name (written in 1967 by Thomas Savage). There are horses, prairies, grizzled cowboys, a title taken from a biblical passage and dead mentors. So far it could be starring John Wayne in 1956. Except the film is directed by Jane Campion, filmed in New Zealand and deals with the fragile nature of male masculinity in a hyper-masculine world. The title is taken from Psalm 22 and the line: "Deliver my soul from the sword; my darling from the power of the dog" is referenced several times throughout. In my opinion, the film takes the concept of *Brokeback Mountain* and does it right. Benedict Cumberbatch gives us a thin, posh Brit and is utterly convincing as a wiry cowpoke, except when his character tries to live up to the legendary masculine ideals of the Old West. This is a man who is clearly struggling to come to terms with his homosexuality.

But it's not just Cumberbatch's show. The four leads, Benedict Cumberbatch, Kirsten Dunst, Jesse Plemons and Kodi Smit-McPhee all shine in this complex adult movie. Part Western, part thriller, part unrequited romance, it is a drama capable of standing up with the best of them. Box office isn't relevant on this occasion as this is an example of Netflix producing prestige content to gain awards and subscribers, an unmistakeable sign that the Western had made it to the streaming era. The movie premiered at the Venice International Film Festival and Campion won the Silver Lion for Best Director. It was nominated for twelve Oscars but only took home one, again it was for Campion as Best Director.

Then in 2024 we get Costner riding in the saddle again with his two-part epic (which was meant to become 3 or 4 but as we shall see this series isn't going to get any more entries) *Horizon: An American Saga*. When the first trailer was launched critics were generally warm to the idea, it looked like people wanted to see a return to classy westerns. But after the premiere in Cannes, the reviews were mixed. A whole generation of film critics had grown up not seeing westerns in the theatre. Many were expecting a revisionist western, instead Costner had created what was in effect the greatest hits of Hawks and Ford conducted with modern film making techniques. Costner, like Wayne before him (with his Alamo movie), put millions of his own money into the project. The first two parts were released in 2024 and were financial disappointments (so much so that the second part still has yet to be released in the UK, at the time of writing, a year later). Perhaps Costner had hoped the fans of *Yellowstone* would turn up, but they didn't and the younger generations were distracted from these genuinely good films by the more obvious fare of *Inside Out 2* and *Deadpool & Wolverine*. Perhaps the series will be finished and be a beautiful Blu-ray box set which will sell well on Father's Day but regardless it's a sign that today, the genre is all but absent from the big screen.

The 21st century shows that the Western isn't going away. Today, it is more likely to be found on the small screen rather than the silver one, but at the same time, it has evolved into anything the creatives want it to be. It could be a prestige project, a comedy, a terrifying thriller. The genre may not be as popular as it was sixty years ago, but it is still part of the conversation.

Conclusion

The Western was there at the start of narrative storytelling in early silent cinema and created household names when the concept of the movie star was in its infancy. When sound was introduced, gun shots were among the first sounds moviegoers heard. Every time there was an innovation in technology or distribution, censorship or social commentary, someone thought the Western would be an appropriate medium to push the boundaries and see where it went.

The interesting thing is that while the genre is not as front of mind as it used to be, it is still, clearly, everywhere. Audiences may no longer be watching Western classics from the 1950s and 60s, but they are watching films that were inspired by those earlier productions. Those who lived in the Wild West are long dead, and the artists who reimagined those stories in the middle of the 20th century are now largely gone too. But it seems as one generation fades another one comes along with enough interest, originality and vision to keep the Western alive.

And now, excuse me, as I take my leave, get on my horse and ride off into the sunset.

If this book has inspired you to watch some more westerns, here's a personal top 10, in no particular order.

The Good, The Bad, and The Ugly
Stagecoach
Dances With Wolves
Once Upon a Time in the West
High Noon
True Grit
Unforgiven
The Great Silence
Butch Cassidy and the Sundance Kid
The Wild Bunch

Dear Reader,

We hope you have enjoyed this book, but why not share your views on social media? You can also follow our pages to see more about our other products: facebook.com/penandswordbooks or follow us on X @penswordbooks

You can also view our products at www.pen-and-sword.co.uk (UK and ROW) or www.penandswordbooks.com (North America).

To keep up to date with our latest releases and online catalogues, please sign up to our newsletter at: www.pen-and-sword.co.uk/newsletter

If you would like a printed catalogue with our latest books, then please email: enquiries@pen-and-sword.co.uk or telephone: 01226 734555 (UK and ROW) or email: uspen-and-sword@casematepublishers.com or telephone: (610) 853-9131 (North America).

We respect your privacy and we will only use personal information to send you information about our products.

Thank you!